Poetry
Of the Heart and
By the Spirit

Jane,
You are a blessing to many. I hope these poems bless you.

Philip Allen Crosby

Philip Allen Crosby

Poetry Of the Heart and by the Spirit Copyright © 2019 by Philip Allen Crosby. All rights reserved. No part of this publication may be reproduced, stored in a retrieval system or transmitted in any way by any means, electronic, mechanical, photocopy, recording or otherwise without the prior permission of the author except as provided by USA copyright law. This novel is a work of fiction. Names, descriptions, entities, and incidents included in the story are products of the author's imagination. Any resemblance to actual persons, events, and entities is entirely coincidental. The opinions expressed by the author are not necessarily those of FWB Publications.

Published by FWB Publications, Columbus, Ohio
Published in the United States of America
ISBN: 9781793249258 Poetry

Christ

Drawn by Dale Crosby

SUBJECT INDEX

CHAPTER ONE - GOD IS LOVE

1. Peace
2. Christian Love
3. Consistent Love
4. People God Created
5. God's Love
6. Suddenly
7. Staying Close
8. Oh, How He Loves You and Me
9. Peace of Mind
   Lost Girl
10. Testimony
11. Live The Faith
12. Time Alone
13. Rain On
14. Circle of Love
    The Love Of Christ
15. Visions
16. I'm Glad The Lord Loves My Soul
17. Thirst For God
    A Happy Ending
18. God Who Loves Us So
    Family Of God
19. The Ten Commandments
20. God's Working
21. No Good Sinner
22. Locked Out
23. Christian Fellowship
24. Adopted Kids
25. All Fed Up
26. I Can Love You
27. Give Love
28. Jesus Is The Answer

CHAPTER TWO - GOD'S FAITHFULNESS

29. God's Harbor Haven
30. Temporary Employee
31. Chicken Dinner Praise
    Friends
32. Law Or Grace
33. Summer's End
34. God Send
35. Continual Care
36. Jesus Train
37. God's Mystery
    God Won't Leave
38. Appreciation
39. Blessed Week
40. Thoughts While Bowling
    It's Just A Game
41. Ephesians
42. Picking Up
    Home
43. He's Always There
44. Tears
45. No Perfect People
46. God's Promises
47. Choose Grace
48. In God We Trust
49. Getting Real
50. Best Of Friends
51. God Can Supply
52. Out Of Debt
53. Trust In The Lord
54. God Knows

CHAPTER THREE - STRUGGLING WITH GOD

55.	Changes	65.	Don't Give Up
56.	For What It's Worth	66.	Drum Temper
57.	Confession	67.	Discontent
58.	God's Math	68.	God's Solution
59.	God's Spirit Is Loving Proof	69.	Tell God Your Frustrations
60.	Mildly Disturbed	70.	Lament
61	Monday Evening	71.	Flicker Faith
62.	Holy Spirit, Don't Leave Me Now	72.	Time With God
63.	Lower Nature	73.	Limits
	Trying Times	74.	Babes In Christ
64.	Out Of Work		

CHAPTER FOUR - OH, HEAR MY PRAYER

75.	Peace With God	91.	Thoughts On Prayer
76.	In His Image	92.	Court Day
77.	Christian Life		Compassion
78.	Lonely	93.	God's Calling
79.	Jail	94.	God Brought Me Here
80.	Pardon Me	95.	Pray About It
81.	Revival	96.	This Thanksgiving Day
82.	One Day I'll See Your Face	97.	When We Feel Gritty
	Claim The Throne	98.	With Thankful Heart, Lord
83.	Repentant Sinner's Heart	99.	The Key
84.	Dependence On God	100.	Brother's Prayer
85.	Blunder Man	101.	Prayer Time
86.	39th Birthday	102.	1986 Year's Review
87.	The Pit	103.	Vacation
88.	Grace	104.	Draw Close To God
89.	Prayer For Healing		
90.	Today's Prayer		
	Fellowship With God		

CHAPTER FIVE - GROWING IN THE SPIRIT

105.	God-Graced Moments	131.	The Parsonage
106.	The Kingdom Of God	132.	Made Whole
107.	Holy Spirit	133.	Green-Haired People
108.	A Holy God	134.	Easy Living
109.	Celebrate Christ	135.	Our Church
110.	Retreat	136.	Transparent
111.	Simple Faith	137.	God's Light
112.	God's Child	138.	Forgiveness
113.	In One Spirit	139.	Amazed By Grace
114.	Good Ol' Folks	140.	Call Jesus
115.	Peace Comes From Within	141.	What's Done For God Just Goes Around
116.	There All Along		
117.	Point Of Reference	142.	Our Life's Work
118.	From Head To Heart	143.	God's Got A Part For You
119.	Vessel Of Love	144.	Condition Covered
120.	Confines	145.	Waiting Till Ready
121.	Expectations	146.	His Spirit Beckons Everyday
122.	Brothers In Christ	147.	God Needs Women
123.	Spirit-Centered Man	148.	We Win
124.	Refreshed	149.	God's Prompting
125.	Good Works	150.	Oriented To God
126.	This Christian Life	151.	Meeting God Together
127.	I Never Noticed	152.	Growing In Amazing Grace
128.	Awakening	153.	Day's End
129.	Clean Living	154.	Just Thinking
130.	My Helper		

CHAPTER SIX - GOD IN NATURE

155.	God's In Charge	167.	Sonlight Breaking Through
156.	God Won't Let Go	168.	The Squirrel
157.	Quiet Time	169.	Smoky
158.	How Falling Leaves Relate To Me	170.	Snow
159.	In Every Season	171.	Icebergs
160.	God's Love Is All Around	172.	Earthquake
161.	Seasons God Made	173.	The Storm
162.	God In Season		Mother Earth
163.	That Sunset Was Really Something	174.	Springtime
			Time Out
164.	The Wind	175.	Choices
165.	Growth In Winter	176.	The Park
166.	Autumn		

CHAPTER SEVEN - MINISTRY TO OTHERS

177. Doing God's Work
178. Bringing Comfort
179. The Right Time
180. On The Rocks
181. Calling Cards
182. Preach The Gospel Everyday.
     If Necessary, Use Words.
     Go
183. Hands Across America
     Reaching Out
184. Imperfection - Still God's Selection
185. It's Not Brainwashing
186. New Hope Church
187. Faithful Living
188. Your Ministry
189. Staff Of Hope
190. Willing Spirit
191. Positioned By God
192. Gospel Singer
193. Choir Of Bells
194. One Hundred Years

CHAPTER EIGHT - CHRISTIAN CELEBRATION

195. Prayerful Christmas
196. What Christmas Means
197. Christmas Road
198. Light Of Christmas
199. Johnston City Christmas
200. Christmas Eve Reflection
201. As Christmas Nears
202. Christmas Once More
203. Blessed New Year
204. God's New Year
205. Hats Off To Moms
206. Mother-Daughter Banquet

CHAPTER NINE - VICTORY IN JESUS

207. What Jesus Means To Me
208. Touched By Jesus
209. Hungry Souls
210. God Came Down
211. The Devil's Lie
212. Heaven's Leaven
213. Being God-Centered
214. Let's Praise The Lord
215. The Lord In My Life
216. Purposed Life
217. Problem Solver
218. Peace In Jesus
219. Living By Faith
220. Clover Fields
221. The Cross
222. Doing What We Can't
223. The River Of Life
224. Holy Spirit Cooking
225. Revival In The Camp
226. There's A Reason I Still Rhyme
227. Happiness
228. Education Reflection
229. Jesus Street
230. In Christ Jesus
231. Purchase Complete
232. Special People
233. God Has Spoken

God Is Love

Chapter One

PEACE

No peace at all
Does this world bring.
No peace at all
In any thing.

The only way
That I have found,
The only way
Peace comes around

Is by loving God,
I'll say it twice:
Is by loving God,
Now ain't that nice?

When God is loved,
We will repent.
When God is loved,
With Him time's spent.

For in God's love
Peace comes about.
For in God's love
There's peace no doubt.

CHRISTIAN LOVE

I want to speak about a love
Which only comes from God above.
It takes root deep within your soul
And gives you warmth like burning coal.
The kind of love I'm speaking of
Once descended like a dove
And found a place within my heart.
When I gave Jesus every part
And knelt down humbly at the cross
And worshipped Christ who paid the cost
Of all the sins I'm guilty of,
He showed forgiveness just because
His grace extended way beyond
The many times that I had wronged
The very One who loves my soul.
In repentance He did make me whole.
Now once we've felt this grace of God,
His Spirit becomes our anchor rod.
We'll feel the peace His love does bring
And worship God and praises sing.
And infused into a sin-filled life,
Is a love and joy which ends the strife.
And when you've chosen to take Christ's hand,
He'll lead you into the Promised Land
And a part of heaven here on earth.
You'll know because you've had rebirth.
Yes, love is what this life's about.
Let Christian love turn you about.

CONSISTENT LOVE

Contrasting moods we all have felt,
From times of joy to times we pout.
God made us so we feel pain
But also warmth from gentle rain.
For we all are living here and now
Connected to God's plan somehow.
And like the seasons which pass by,
We're born, we live, and then we die.
But just as death contrasts with life,
A peace exists beneath the strife.
Though moods and situations change,
One thing I'd never rearrange
Is how God who made it all
Loves each person, big or small.
No matter if we love Him back,
He still loves us, and that's a fact.
For life exists because of God,
And His love for us we cannot rob.
For unlike we who vacillate,
Our Lord shows love and never hate.
Consistently for our own good
He waits to help whoever would
Call on Him in time of need
And listen to an earnest plea.
The Holy Spirit still exists
To comfort us when life does twist
And plays a sort of cruel joke
To humankind, and, yes, His folk.
For believing souls still face life's test,
But in the end, with Jesus rest.
And contrasting moods don't count as much
As consistent faith in the Master's touch.

PEOPLE GOD CREATED

The Lord it's true I do believe
In giving life, in us did weave
Connected with our very breath
A part of Him, alive and fresh.
For God, whose love for every soul,
Each person, God created whole.
No two people just the same,
God knows indeed each person's name.
And because God's love we can't escape,
Even if we're filled with hate;
Even if we've done all wrong
And then sadly we don't have a song.
When all the world it seems has turned
Against us and our sin has burned
So deeply that it's left a scar,
Even then God's not off far.
For if we'll just confess our shame
And pray to God in Jesus' name
That He would fill, renew, and shape
This one who's strayed and caused heartache.
Yes, you and I and all the rest
Till serving God, we're not the best.
Until our eyes, which once were closed
In spirit speaking, we had dozed;
Until that time and not before,
We miss what God has made us for.
To love and serve and do His will,
And spread His love to others till
The beauty of each precious soul,
As formed at birth again is whole.
And God will help us in this task
If daily we will only ask
That He will show us what to do
And give us wisdom to renew
The seeds of love placed in our heart.
The day it dawned we are a part
Of a work that God put forth in love
And is with us now from up above.

GOD'S LOVE

Such a love God has for us all.
He sent a Savior born in a stall.
His Word became flesh because we wouldn't hear it.
Jesus was born of a virgin by the Holy Spirit.
Glorious Lord, He knew the heart of man.
Laws convicted; follow if you can.
He knew we needed human example.
Revealed self in Christ; Holy sample.
True to His word, prophecy fulfilled.
His own Son sent into the world and killed.
Slain for the sins of people such as me.
Calvary's ultimate sacrifice hung on a tree.
All to show thick-headed folks,
Who think they're cool because they've learned the ropes,
That there is a God who cares all about them,
Who doesn't give up when we're lost in sin.
He sent Jesus to show us how He loves,
Free grace not conditioned on what one does.
A love that encompasses more than we hoped for,
That we not be lost He holds open the door.
A just God who hears all our wailings,
We can turn to Him for forgiveness of our failings.
Life will have its adversities a blowing;
Assurance comes from God's love a knowing.
His love lights a candle inside,
Shining to others as in Him we abide.
Jesus has spoken to the hearts of the masses.
Under the blood He'll forgive our trespasses,
Scrubbing us clean from a dirty nature.
He tugs at our heart and offers a cure.
God does not want a soul to be lost.
That's why He paid the incredible cost,
A fee that was paid to show His great love.
Thank you, Lord, for the heavenly shove.
Thank you, Lord, for speaking to my heart.
Born again, my life has a new start.
I may not know what tomorrow will bring,
But His love for me gives reason to sing.
All my hopes and concerns for tomorrow
Are shared by the Father through good times and sorrow.
God gave us life and will walk by our side.
Just praise and seek Him; do not hide.
A new life not dependent on the action of others,
His love within we're everyone's brother.
So thanks again, Lord, for your bountiful grace.
In Jesus, Lord, we see your face.

SUDDENLY

Suddenly my sin forgiven,
Suddenly a kind of living
I had never known before.
Opened up, and through the door
A world of love and grace unearned
Enveloped me the more I learned.
Suddenly while on my knees,
A broken vessel, if you please,
Crying out, "Oh, Lord, I'm wrong!"
So in need I had no song.
Suddenly it came together.
God loved me beyond all measure.
Doing everything He could
To draw us closer as we should,
To see that He was always there,
And I was always in His care.
Suddenly the pieces fit.
Salvation, every bit of it
Was done when Christ died on the cross;
Unblemished lamb of God the cost
To pay the debt I couldn't pay.
All grace, His love the only way
To touch my heart and let me see
What Jesus did He did for me.
A new birth basically that hour,
Babe in Christ just like a flower
That is connected to the vine.
All praise to God the Lord is mine.
And just as suddenly I saw
His love had freed me from the law.
And all that I could ever do
Is share that love with folks like you
And pray that suddenly your heart
Will let Christ enter every part.

STAYING CLOSE

Where Christ abides I have seen
The sweetest spirit, never mean.
When on my own and out of touch,
I reflect the world and as such
I'm very likely to fall down
And walk around with a frown.
So why on earth are we prone
To ever want to walk alone
When we are witness to the truth?
The Lord has helped us since our youth.
Even when we sought Him not,
He still reached out to save our lot.
And so today I must say thanks
That I'm included in the ranks
Of people God has great love for;
His grace just makes me love Him more.
For in myself I see each day
Where naturally there'd be no way
That I could ever earn God's love.
We both know sins I'm guilty of.
An act of faith let me decide
That love for me God didn't hide.
For its been there all along,
And if not received it's I who's wrong.
So, Lord, I'm trying to walk close;
Beyond this world I need You most.
And, Lord, I pray your love will stay
Within my spirit every day.

OH, HOW HE LOVES YOU AND ME

God loves me;
This I know
For the Bible tells me so.
What about you?

Why love me?
My sins show...
Unworthy as any foe...
Describe you, too?

But for love a fee
God paid it - not me!
His Son hung on a tree.

God loves me;
This I know.
'Tis grace which makes it so.
Am I reaching you?

Rotten as I can be
God wants me to grow.
By prayer the sin will go.
Ask Him - be made new.

It's by grace - not me.
God paid it - it's free.
Oh, how He loves you and me!

God asks, "Got love for me?"
Doesn't matter if we're low,
He cares. His seed in us He will sow
Forgiveness - cleans clear through.

Do open your Bible. It's the key.
By the Spirit it was written for us to see.
Oh, how He loves you and me!

PEACE OF MIND

What can give you peace of mind
And bring you through the tightest bind,
When all around is gloom and strife
And cutting spirits with their knife?
The only answer to this query
In a world that's old and often weary
Is to keep your purpose stayed on Thee;
To love the Lord and be set free.
When all seems lost and no hope we see,
The Lord will honor our fidelity.
For without our faith we can't please God,
He wants to be our anchor rod.
And when all our burdens we cast on Jesus,
His Spirit comes; it doesn't leave us.
We know to trust for we have learned
His grace suffices; it's not earned.
And when at last we see some light,
We know who held us in the night.
And this assurance of God's love
Brings the peace of mind I'm speaking of.

LOST GIRL

It's apparent to all we've a beautiful day,
So why should we notice the rot and decay?
See the girl walking by with the smile on her face?
Never know it by looking, but she's a sad case.
She once had it all; a husband and child.
Now they're taken from her, and she has turned wild.
Her smile just conceals a hurt deep within;
Now she's always alone and yet everyone's friend.
Yes, it's true. God has made us a beautiful world,
But if He's not in your life, the devil's unfurled.
So, yes, we need to give praise to God
And thank Him each day as we walk on His sod.
Let us reach out to the girl who is lost;
The help we provide will outweigh the cost.
For only by giving of God's love we enjoy
Will the gospel of hope reach each girl and boy.

TESTIMONY

My testimony,
What I've learned
The things God's done for me...
I know it well,
And I must tell
So others, too, can see.

For it's not phony
And it's not earned—
The things God's done for me.
But I think it swell,
Really rang my bell,
And at last has set me free.

And your testimony,
It's not burned
The things God's done for you.
So I do impel:
Do not undersell,
But just simply speak words true.

For your testimony
What you've discerned,
The things God's done for you,
Only you can tell
For you know it well,
And you'll find that when you do

That a hearer stony
Who's to God not turned
For the things God can supply,
Heading straight for hell
Going there pell-mell
May begin to question why.

Why their testimony
Of the things they've learned?
Lacks the things God can supply,
Because once they fell,
Darkness did indwell,
And life seemed to pass them by.

So by our testimony,
What we've learned
The things God's done for us,
To the mademoiselle
Or a Jezebel
This can be the impetus

To start a testimony
Of a life that's turned
And opened to things God's done.
Because His personnel,
A former infidel,
Sharing God's love, souls have been won.

And by our testimony
Of this love not earned
And all the things that God has done,
We do God's will.
May faith grow until
Others see in us God's Son.

LIVE THE FAITH

Do people question what you say
Or listen to your words today?
Your witness, friend, I'm speaking of.
Does it exhibit Jesus' love?
No one's perfect, that's for sure;
And most times few of us are pure.
We say and do things we should not,
And often times in fact we're caught.
We're no way perfect like God's Son,
But in this world is anyone?
The Lord says we've all fallen short,
But God through mercy's not the sort
To fail to give unending love
To His redeemed from up above.
From all around through Holy Spirit
God's so near; oh, can't you hear it?
His still, sweet presence, is by your side.
Your every need to Him confide.
Tell the Lord your hopes and fears.
Confess your sins; He'll dry your tears.
A God of love who knows you well,
Who by His grace sent Christ to tell
Fallen mankind that God forgives.
The ransom's paid, in Christ one lives
Life to the fullest, never alone,
A friend much closer than the phone.
Can people see the Christ you know
By how you live, does His light show?
Your witness should be more than words;
Without God's love it's for the birds.
Showing grace like you've received
Exalts the Lord, be not deceived.
Our witness will be only talk
Unless with Christ we walk the walk;
To keep us close, divine protection,
Have prayer each day for His direction.
Our witness then the Lord will bless,
For faith in Christ can do no less.

TIME ALONE

I've had some time to be alone,
And this, in part, is why I've grown.
My faith has deepened just because
When my world ended, God gave me love.
A firm assurance I received.
It'll all work out, once I believed
That God almighty really cares,
And He in fact answers prayers.
There's not a reason to give up hope,
For what concerns me is in His scope.
My children now are far away;
I pray each day they'll be OK.
I've been wronged, but with God's help
I've found forgiveness and have felt
A kind of peace which only comes
When I've turned over all the ones
I care about into God's trust.
I know I've done then what I must.

RAIN ON

Into every life some rain must pour.
Some folks have little and others more.
Problems seem inherent in the lives of men;
Opportunities of faith or pathways to sin.
Are you up to your neck in the problems of life?
Is this chaotic world causing you strife?
Do you toss and turn and lose sleep at night,
And from sunup to sundown this life's a fight?
Well, my friend, I hope it's not that bad.
I have some news which can make you glad.
You have a part in the Kingdom of God.
Just trust in the Lord as you walk on His sod.
When your soul, mind, and spirit are fixed on the Lord,
You're renewed in the power of love's sweet accord.
You can look at your problems from a better point of view,
And the Lord will help you with what you should do.
Some problems are stubborn and seem without solution;
But turned over to God, even these bring fruition.
You can't stop the rain from coming your way,
But sheltered in God's love will help you to say,
"I love you, Lord, and seek Your will in my life—
A clear direction, not throwing the dice."

CIRCLE OF LOVE

Enlarge the circle of your love.
Reach out with guidance from above.
Let God's love fill your cup
And keep your thought waves looking up.
And as the circle of God's love
Expands through you to people of
A more diverse and complex lot,
You'll find more often times than not
That you'll be treated back the same
With love and kindness in the main.
For people like a friendly soul,
Especially one our Lord's made whole.
So let your loving circle grow,
And you'll be blessed this much I know.

THE LOVE OF CHRIST

The love of Christ makes life complete;
To serve Him makes your life more sweet.
To struggle seems to be man's lot.
God knows us well; He's not forgot
That we are weak and sinful bound.
We need His Spirit all around,
To save us from our selfish selves.
To be set free in us He dwells.
To those who earnestly repent,
They accept as Savior the Son He sent.
And if we pray in Jesus' name,
For sure we'll never be the same.
Our sights will be on higher goals.
We'll love the Maker of our soul.
Our daily actions will reveal
The love inside us is for real.
It's come from God who's met our need,
To dwell on Him, our soul to feed.

VISIONS

As through the haze of early morn,
In fog-like vision memories torn
From pages written of my life,
So many of them filled with strife.
I look back now, and I recall,
Not perfectly, but still somehow,
What sticks out most are seasons when
Adventures started to begin.
Like newfound love that felt so good
And scouting ventures chopping wood,
When I was not afraid at all
Of winter's bleakness past the fall
Because I had there in the night
A faithful lover to hold tight.
The memories of my kids when small
Remind me I once had it all—
Or so I thought until one day
The love of God was felt my way.
And on that day, the visions clear.
My Lord, I felt You, oh, so near.
And it was quickened to my soul
Without you God I'm just not whole.
Now other visions cross my mind
Of harder times that were unkind.
But when in circumstances black,
When needing God I didn't lack.
For every earnest prayer's been heard.
I'm claiming Jesus at the Word.

I'M GLAD THE LORD LOVES MY SOUL

I'm so tired of being alone.
My wife no more will even phone.
And the load I carry makes me groan.
I'm glad the Lord loves my soul.

This life sometimes makes me cry.
When all goes wrong, I wonder why.
To say I'm happy would be a lie.
I'm glad the Lord loves my soul.

This bit of news warms my heart.
His love gives me the boost to start,
A life of faith to live and chart.
I'm glad the Lord loves my soul.

I know I've sinned so many times.
If not for mercy, I'd join the lines
That lead to hell and untold fines.
I'm glad the Lord loves my soul.

The Lord above is more than fair.
He sent Jesus to show He cares.
He will forgive us I've become aware.
I'm glad the Lord loves my soul.

And though the problems seem to never end,
God's Spirit puts my spirit on the mend.
I rejoice because the Lord is my friend.
I'm glad the Lord loves my soul.

THIRST FOR GOD

There're things about me you don't know.
Sometimes my spirit runs on low.
There're times my witness goes to hell,
And many, many times I fall.
And yet I must confess to you,
With all the things that I've been through,
I don't regret one little bit,
And pray I'll never want to quit
The longing deep within my heart
To serve my Lord and do my part.
And this because I'll have you know
The love of God is what's made me whole.
His love, praise God, was poured on me,
And spirit eyes, once blind, could see
The day I knelt in humble prayer
And asked that Jesus meet me there.
And on that day, and ever since
I've had a thirst the world can't quench.
And that, my friend, is nothing more
Than Jesus with me to the core.

A HAPPY ENDING

They all just want a happy ending—
The mass of people all around.
What kind of signal are we sending?
Does the life we're living let love abound?

A happy ending is a swell goal,
And no one likes a long face.
But we're not always on a roll,
And sad times often stalk our place.

The happy ending we are after,
At times seems but a silly dream.
But if we'll live to serve the Master,
We'll know a joy that's felt and seen.

For when we think on what God's done—
All of creation and His love—
Then our happy ending is not just fun,
But it's sharing our life with God above.

GOD WHO LOVES US SO

Oh, people, ain't it nice to know
There is a God who loves us so—
A God who shows abundant grace
And cares about the woes we face?
Oh, people, I'm not blowing air.
The Lord I've found does really care.
For every weary soul in need
He sent us Jesus here to feed
Our souls with life; to clear our head,
Born again, no longer dead.
So we can see that God loves us.
Doesn't matter that we missed the bus,
Doesn't matter that we made a mess,
He will forgive if we confess.
He will restore and make us right,
If we'll love Him with all our might.
If we'll praise God, He will restore
A life disrupted to the core.
He healed my life and opened doors.
Oh, people, let Him heal yours.

FAMILY OF GOD

I'm so glad I'm a part of the family of God.
I've been washed in the fountain, cleansed by His blood.
Joint heirs with Jesus as we travel this sod,
I'm so glad I'm a part of the family of God.
And as a part of the family of God,
Think what you will, I may seem odd.
But I've discovered way deep in my soul,
This is the family that's made me whole.
All praise to Jesus for this family of mine,
A royal household of the best line.
Those in this family show God's great love;
Praise God He's touched us from above.
Growing and serving, in the palm of His hand,
Each day worth living, now isn't that grand?
Let me repeat what is my anchor rod:
I'm so glad I'm a part of the family of God.

THE TEN COMMANDMENTS

The Ten Commandments once were written
For a lost humanity deep in sin,
That they might know what's right and fit'n
To please the Lord and enter in.

To His own Kingdom here on earth
The way was shown, engraved on stone.
It was more than rules; it gave new birth.
The Lord sought we should be His own.

That we should place no god before Him
And we should worship Him alone,
With all our hearts, a song, a hymn;
In all our ways let love be shown.

When our love and purpose are stayed on Thee,
Then we'll treat our neighbors like ourselves.
And ourselves we'll love for we can see
That the God we love within us dwells.

And that's the part of the Kingdom of God
That the Ten Commandments revealed to us.
That in all our days as this earth we've trod,
The Lord is with us from birth to dust.

Though on our own a sinful lot,
Praise God He loves us all the while.
When we repent, with God we've got
A life worth living and a smile.

GOD'S WORKING

Grunting, growing, and moaning;
Working hard, try'n to make it.
But hardest effort pays little reward
Unless Christ is in it and you're thanking the Lord.

Lifting, bending, and straining;
Starting early - takes a lot of grit.
Prices high - more than I can afford,
But thanks to Jesus, I've got the Lord.

All this work, sometimes feel like fainting;
Come on payday, I'll sure take it.
Variety of bills, ya never get bored—
Glad the Lord loves me - Jesus the cord.

No artist, can't make it painting;
Gotta work, gotta do my bit.
Family needs me, might say I'm moored.
Thanks God, when I leave here we'll be on the same ward.

God loves me, such peace just in knowing;
Feel Him all around me, like a ball in a mitt,
All by grace, not what I deserve;
Praise you Lord. I want to serve.

Yes, seems like the worlds pressures are growing,
But Christ living in me helps me get through it.
Working, yet happy, my head a hollow gourd?
No , friend, just smiling, all thanks to my Lord.

NO GOOD SINNER

Some truths are hard for us to see.
We sleep till we have need of Thee.
It takes for most a sudden jolt
Perhaps our world to unbolt
To see more clearly who we are,
And that our Lord is not off far.
A truth that's always hard to face
In every life, in any place,
Is that my sin is all no good.
Yes, no good sinner ever could
Save himself from Satan's grip,
Just wanting to won't do the trick.
And many folks have been deceived;
Their sin was little they believed.
In fact they've thought a hundred times
That God will overlook their crimes,
Not seeing they are in great need
Of Jesus Christ to take the lead,
To let His love become their own,
To guide so they are not alone.
And sometimes God will bring us to
A place where nothing else will do.
We will either self-destruct
Or in a moment be awestruck
When two things happen all at once.
When born again no more a dunce,
We see ourselves for what we are:
A no good sinner from God far.
And when we cry that God forgive,
His grace that moment lets us live.
We're awestruck by God's love for us;
We're not an undeserving cuss.
But that's the reason for the joy:
Christ died to save this wretched boy.
He died that you and I might live,
Abundantly with much to give.
By trusting in God's precious Son
We see most clearly He's the One;
The light, the truth, the only way
That you or I can be OK.

LOCKED OUT

What if we were not allowed,
Or worse yet, maybe felt too proud
To worship God out in the open,
And Jesus' name could not be spoken.
Wouldn't it be quite a shame
If to a service no one came
Because they knew that they'd be seen,
And to some folks that isn't keen?
For some who think they know us well,
And many faults they sure could tell,
And if they chose to press the matter
Might succeed our faith to shatter.
And if we're not full of God's Word,
And it's not sunk in the truth we've heard,
That even though we have clay feet,
On a cross sin met defeat.
Not allowed to praise God's name,
The once lost captive not the same,
You and I who've seen the light
Will not return into the night.
We've sunk down low enough to sink,
But Jesus saved us from the brink.
He saved us from the sin within
And built a bridge, now God is kin.
We can worship in our heart
The Lord who saved us, every part.
And as a people who know Him
Let His peace show in our grin.
Let our lives become a temple
Of God's grace, so sweet and simple.
We don't need to know it all
We give God thanks. We heard His call,
For God loved us a long, long time;
He loved us when we sank into slime.
So we should never be so proud
That we can't praise God right out loud.
And even if the chapel's locked,
Praise in our hearts just can't be stopped.

CHRISTIAN FELLOWSHIP

Welcome to this fellowship.
No one's perfect, we all slip,
But there is joy here all because
We've learned to lean on Jesus' love.
Far more constant than we are,
God's grace, a bright and shining star.
When we repent, ask God forgive
His healing touch does let us live.
So in this fellowship we find
Strength and joy and peace of mind.
We can drop the curtain down,
Express our hurt; and all around
Brothers and sisters in the Lord
Extend themselves and come on board,
Helping us to struggle through,
In God's Spirit something new.
A fresh anointing floods our souls;
The Devil's lies are full of holes
For we're reminded in this place
God's love exceeds what all we face;
That we now have a caring friend
Who'll stick by us until the end.
This fellowship, a place to pray,
Meets our needs and shows a way.
That even in our darkest hours
God's people nurture, and like flowers,
The sweet aroma of their care
Makes us certain God is there.
For this is how the good Lord chose
To spread His Kingdom for He knows
For people to see Christ as real
His love imparted they must feel.
And it's in fellowships like ours,
Jesus, healer of our scars,
Comes alive and all because
We feel the presence of His love.

ADOPTED KIDS

We're adopted by God's grace
Into His family once we face
The truth that we are bound by sin
Until we ask Christ enter in.
All glory to the Son of Man.
He makes us worthy, says we can
Join the family of His love.
God's Kingdom we're partakers of.
Not bound by law, in faith we see
What Jesus did, He did for me.
Heirs to God's amazing grace,
Adopted in, we take our place
As members of God's family.
Abraham, we're of His tree.
And as a member of the clan.
God's promises, part of the plan
Apply to you and apply to me.
And praise God's name we are set free
From Satan's bondage over us!
Adopted kids, our Lord we trust
For it's God's Spirit in control.
It's Jesus Christ who's made us whole.

Galatians 4:4-5
Romans 8:16-17

ALL FED UP

Are you fed or just fed up?
So much depends on if your cup
Is filled each day with things of God
Or mired in this old earthly sod.
Heaven minded some may claim,
Thrilled and touched at Jesus' name.
Taking in the bread of life,
Bible study with your wife,
Concentrating on God's love,
Praising Him, with hands above.
These are people kept alive
With faith in God, and so they thrive.
Not that life is always kind,
But with the Lord a peace they find.
Jesus loves me, this I know;
Think about it when you're low.
We are all part of His plan.
When Spirit-filled He says we can
Overcome the world's snare,
And in His love we'll find we care
Deeply for the hurts of others.
New found friends we count as brothers.
Why? Because when God is first,
Pleasing Him does quench our thirst
As nothing in the world will.
We're just fed up, that is until
It strikes us in a profound way
God's love transforms our night to day.
So, friend, if you are just fed up
And count your lot to be bad luck,
And contemplate some drastic measure,
Listen, pilgrim, I have treasure.
It comes clearly from the Lord—
His Word, His Spirit, moving toward
The place where it can do some good.
It's in your heart, and Jesus could
Turn a fed-up critic to
A God-fed saint washed clean and new.
The choice, my friend, is all your call.
Consider giving Christ your all.

I CAN LOVE YOU

Don't tell me I can't love you,
For that's the choice I make.
Don't tell me I can't love you,
For there's a lot at stake.

To start with, you're important,
For God gave life to you.
To start with its important,
For God says this to do.

God says to love each other
As He has love for us.
God says to love each other
Without a lot of fuss.

We need not be a life-long pal
To demonstrate God's love.
We need not be a life-long pal
To share what we're made of.

And if by grace forgiven
For our ungodly deeds,
And once by grace forgiven,
Can't help to where this leads.

For, brother, it puts joy inside
To share with souls like you.
For, brother, when there's joy inside,
By Christ we're made brand new.

So, yes, in Christ I love you,
For He has made me whole.
So, yes, in Christ I love you,
For you're a special soul.

For, brother, you are just like me,
For God loves you the same.
For, brother, it's for souls like we,
Christ died and bore our shame.

GIVE LOVE

I'm told I'm soft because I cry
From time to time, and that a guy
Shouldn't let the world see
The naked, sentimental me.
It's not the proper thing to do.
But, brother, if you only knew
How hard and distant I had been,
I doubt that you would like me then.
I kept emotions closely guarded;
Feelings could get something started.
Didn't have the time for that;
Keep things light and we can chat.
But don't go deep where pain is found;
I wouldn't want to be around.
I guess I had a hardened soul.
The problems in life took its toll.
But as a man I had my pride;
A good front meant that I could hide
Behind this mask of self-control.
But that could never make me whole.
For me it took a lot of time
To come to terms with my own crime.
I thought that I could do it all.
A fool— I hadn't heard God's call.
I hadn't given Him much thought.
Oh, sure, the gospel I'd been taught.
But me a sinner, lost and bound,
I couldn't see; I wasn't found.
I hadn't met the risen Lord.
That is, till one day, grace was poured
Over me from head to toes.
God saw my need, and heaven knows
The tears flowed freely on that day.
My spirit eyes saw right away
Apart from God there is no peace.
Confessing, turning, sweet release
Came that day, I'm not ashamed.
I cry for happy, Jesus named
Me friend and member of His clan.
A love so deep that all I can
Is thank Him daily with how I live.
Love freely given, love freely given.

JESUS IS THE ANSWER

Jesus is the answer
For the world today.
Without Him all is cancer;
Hear what He has to say.
A happy life pays a cost;
Give of yourself much love.
Forgive and reach out to the lost;
Seek our Father from above.
The world shuns this kind of thinking.
Get even and settle the score,
And then by golly start to drinking,
Creating a world of darkness more and more.
This is a life many find
Who listen to the Devil's talk,
But if you keep Jesus on your mind
You'll be strutting in your walk.
If you think this foolish chatter,
You've not met the risen Lord.
God loves us and we really matter.
Praise God for Jesus the cord.
For in the life of Christ the man,
We see what God is really like:
A God of love with a perfect plan.
At the cross we drove the spike,
For God loves us even when
Our lives are far outside His will.
What separates us is our sin,
And sin is darkness than can kill.
Without Christ in our lives,
We become our own worst enemy.
For without His love, darkness thrives;
That's why Christ says, "Come to me.
I am the way,
The truth and the light.
Come to me," Jesus did say,
"And I will guide and give you sight."
You will see more than before,
Reborn in Christ, a new beginning;
The Comforter will help you more and more,
And soon new souls you'll be winning.

God's Faithfulness

Chapter Two

God's Harbor Haven

I've got confidence
God's going to see me through.
No matter what the case may be,
He's going to fix it for me.
I'm in no trance;
With Jesus skies are blue.

A sweet song inside
Is there because I belong,
For the Lord is always by my side.
In deep waters His shoulder is wide.
Forget your selfish pride;
Let Jesus be your song.

The joy of the Lord
Is the strength of my life.
Hills and valleys sometimes are steep,
But at peace with Jesus I can sleep.
For with the King I am moored;
His harbor haven calms the strife.

I can choose to walk alone,
But I've learned the Lord loves to help.
In all things we should pray,
And let Him show us the way.
In our praise His light is shown,
And in our prayers His love is felt.

The Holy Spirit is my director.
Let me be a vessel God can use.
Help me rise above life's woes
And spread God's light to those He chose.
For I'm a sinner who's entered His door,
Loved in grace despite my abuse.

And, oh, what a difference
God's love for me has made!
Now when life's troubles come my way,
I know whose voice I shall obey.
My Lord wants me not on the fence
But to share His love which will never fade.

TEMPORARY EMPLOYEE

I took a job that's temporary;
Short duration, kind of scary,
Knowing income soon would end
If help from God He didn't send.
Living each day to the max,
You know on faith there is no tax.
For when you're going day by day,
Trusting God in every way
That all your needs will be supplied.
Secure our Lord will never hide
His love and mercy and His care
To those who call on Him in prayer.
Then you can save a lot of grief
That worry brings with unbelief.
Christ calls us sons, heirs of the King.
He doesn't hold back anything
That isn't really for our best.
He beckons come enter in His rest.
That's not to say we don't work hard.
We press ahead, each foot, each yard,
Knowing in the end we'll find
Just what we knew, that God is kind.

CHICKEN DINNER PRAISE

Chomping down a chicken dinner,
Thinking Lord you are a winner.
All is good that You have made.
Right now I thank You for this shade.
This has been a long hard day,
And I've not taken time to pray.
But as I chew this chicken bone,
I think on all the love You've shown.
You are the lover of my soul;
How much perhaps I'll never know.
Last night You cared to give me rest.
Today with You I'm once more blessed.
You have provided to save my life.
One day I pray You'll save my wife.
For You have helped me weather every storm;
What's good inside me, You helped form.
Oh, how I know I've caused You grief,
But that You love me is my belief.
When my life starts on the wrong route,
Your Holy Spirit turns me about.
I thank You, Lord, you've made me aware
That though I stumble, You still care.

FRIENDS

Lord, in You how I've been blessed!
Your love has helped me pass each test.
When I look back on this year past,
A smile comes to me really fast.
For I see faces that I've met
That have been a blessing, you can bet.
They're people, Lord, who just like me
Have such a need, Lord, just for Thee.
And when we gather in Christ's name,
In spirit we become the same.
We're all God's children, it's so clear,
In Christ, together, gone is fear.
These friends, my Lord, I thank you for.
In You there's not a one that's poor.
And I am richer here today
Because these friends have come my way.

LAW OR GRACE

Law or grace, which will you choose?
There's only one which is good news.
To do what's right because we must;
Begrudging service without trust;
Laws and rules, which to bend;
Prayers so short, no time to spend.
Laws are needed I suppose;
Without them chaos, Heaven knows.
But laws can only do so much
For those whose lives they daily touch.
They cannot bring a change of heart,
Nor make us want to do our part
Except to face a certain fine;
Obeyed perhaps but then we whine.
A change of heart, grace enter in.
We see ourselves as full of sin.
We recognize that our Creator
Has a plan that is much greater
Than all our laws or sin could be.
God paid a price for you and me.
He sacrificed His very best:
His Son who aced on every test;
Whose love reflected all God's glory;
To die, then live to tell the story.
An act of grace on our estate,
It shows in God's Book how we rate.

God cared enough to let us know
Where we are He, too, will go.
That He will never leave us stranded,
Grace and love, together banded;
Armor from the throne of God;
His strength with us, an anchor rod.
Christ, the grace I'm speaking of,
With His Spirit we feel God's love.
Now which to choose, it sounds so easy;
Grace calls out that we can please Thee.
When we're led now by the Spirit,
We'll do what's right. Oh, we can hear it.
God's direction in our lives,
For better husbands, better wives.
For God's grace opens up the door;
We know now who we're living for;
The One who's loved us all along.
Forgiven—thanks, God, for the song
You've entered into our heart of hearts;
Grace enough for all the parts
That make a life so worth the living,
Each day with Him is now Thanksgiving.
Choosing law won't give this peace.
Praise God His grace is our release.

SUMMERS END

As I sit on this nice green lawn,
I think about where my summer's gone.
Some days were, oh, so very hot,
But by in large they were not.
Compared to many summers past,
This one for me I wish could last.
The lengthened days of this time of year
Have warmed my heart to something clear.
That if we trust God when all seems lost,
He'll stay by our side however we're tossed.
A summer's gone by without the ones I love,
But God has provided with help from above.
I can no longer count on the one I married,
But I can count on the Lord in whose arms I'm carried.
These long summer days have been busy and active;
The Lord's been beside me to make them attractive.
For without God's love in my heart taking root,
Asked for what I could praise, I'd become mute.
I thank God I've been close to the King of all ages.
Life's so much sweeter than the sum of my wages.
Summer is ending, but there are new beginnings.
In which ever season with Christ we are winning.

GODSEND

Whom will God send
To our aid?
Whom will God send?
Lord we've prayed.

It's been uphill
For awhile.
It's been uphill
And hard to smile.

And Lord we know
You see our need.
And Lord we know
In us Your seed,

Of trust and hope
Is planted there.
Of trust and hope,
We know You care.

And You'll provide;
We count it done.
And You'll provide
For such a one.

A Godsend now,
Oh, could it be?
A Godsend now,
Is it you or me?

CONTINUAL CARE

Every detail, every spot
Of our lives, God cannot
Help but really care about;
Of this fact I have no doubt.
We may well be unaware
Of our Lord's continual care.
So we stagger on our own,
Babes in Christ, not fully grown,
Thinking only matters grim
Are enough to interest Him.
Like when all but hope is gone,
In desperation it does dawn
In our minds, Lord, I need help.
But listen. It's not how you felt
At that moment or before.
Christ waits always at the door,
Ready that you seek His grace;
That no one else should take His place.
Friends sometimes just can't be found,
But Christ will always be around,
There to hear you're every prayer
And every secret that you share.
Broken heart or joyous song,
In any case you do belong
To the One who loves your soul.
Communion is what makes you whole.
Knowing that the Lord of All
Came to earth, born in a stall,
And lived a sinless life as man,
Sacrificed so we all can
Share His glory through our lives;
Boys and girls, husband's wives.
We can because the Lord of Hosts
Loves you and me the very most,
And by His rising from the grave,
The battle's won! He truly saves!

JESUS TRAIN

Step right up and come aboard.
This train's about to leave.
Tickets paid by the Lord,
So come and don't you grieve.

There're joy and peace aboard this train
That's moving right on track.
There's help in time of grief and strain
And power given when you lack.

This train's conductor is never wrong;
He knows your every need.
Your sins confessed to Him are gone;
Through troubles He will lead.

The Holy Spirit feeds this train
And all who climb on board,
And cleanses all and every stain
Of those who love the Lord.

I pray that you will find the gate.
It's narrow, some say small.
But once you've entered, gone is hate
When Christ becomes your all.

The train I speak of has much room
For you and all your friends.
It's leaving scheduled sometime soon,
So hurry lest it ends.

And bring on board as many souls
As you can so inspire;
For the Jesus train has worthy goals,
And it is God's great desire.

GOD'S MYSTERY

God has ways to us mysterious,
Grace sufficient when we're furious.
Time and time again He tries,
Though we're unwilling, to make us wise.
He'll let us fall flat on our face
At times in point to make a case
That without Him our plan will fail;
But even so He'll post our bail.
For while it's true we don't deserve;
In fact to ask requires some nerve.
The kind of love and grace He shows,
All we need He clearly knows,
It goes to prove how great Thou Art;
Revealed self to us impart.
A portion of His grace and love,
His mystery from up above;
That we are worthy in God's sight;
His grace a mystery to make us right.
But, brother, it's faith on our part
That allows God's mystery into our hearts.

GOD WON'T LEAVE

I need you, Lord, now more than ever.
It's by faith I'm held together.
Faith you love this struggling soul;
Faith your prayer that I be whole.
A kind of freedom we achieve
When by your Spirit we believe
That we're held safely in your fold.
You'll be around when we are old.
And all the times we seek you out,
You'll never leave, I have no doubt.

APPRECIATION

Don't we all, if truth be known,
Wish some light on seeds we've sown
Would be exalted, lifted high
And folks would smile as we walk by?
For at the center don't we all
Like to walk with our head tall
And think the sacrifice we made
In appreciation debt be paid?
Yes, appreciation is appreciated,
More so if it's long you've waited.
For a firm handshake and word of thanks
As human beings surely rank
Among the pleasures we rank high.
And don't you know the reason why?
Because we all do seek a place
Where we may gladly show our face
And have assurance we are loved,
A place respected we're not shoved.
And, friend, I think that you will find
In Jesus Christ the very kind
Of understanding, grace and love
That appreciation's so full of.
And once it's sunk down in your soul
The price God paid to make you whole;
Your debt of sin that God's Son paid,
Upon a cross that we had made —
Then what others think and say
Won't matter that much anyway.
For we'll thank God for what He's done,
Appreciating God's own Son.
And as we serve Him by His grace,
An appreciated God we'll face,
And in the judgment God will say,
"Well done, good servant. Come My way."

BLESSED WEEK

I've been blessed this week for sure.
All praise to God, He is the cure.
When I was tired and worn out
With Christian people poured the fount
Of blessings God chose to give.
It works that way. We see Christ live
When He is needed and He's sought.
You'll find Him, but He can't be bought.
For Christ responds to prayer and praise.
When He is welcome then He stays.
The Holy Spirit lifted me;
Ask my wife, she will agree.
And then I saw God work things out
That only He could bring about.
People walking in His steps,
Doing God's work by the text;
Giving freely all because
God has touched them with His love.
But greater still I do believe
We're service pledges folks did leave
On the altar of the church.
Given time and prayer to search
Their hearts for what Christ calls them to,
Commitments saying this I'll do
For You my Lord because I see
You've paid the highest price for me.
You've done the work; it's now complete.
What's good rests only at your feet.
In your service Lord this week
You've blessed and made me more complete.

THOUGHTS WHILE BOWLING

We smoke because we're nervous;
We drink because we're blue.
We worry about tomorrow;
Our lives are full of sorrow.
These traits don't really serve us.
So what's a man to do?

So long as man's existed
Like problems have enveloped
Mortal souls against the wall
Who on their own can't help but fall.
For the rightful order has been twisted.
So in the dark, dim lives developed.

Just looking through the natural eye
Makes a free soul blue.
We need to look with faith to God,
Not caring if folks find us odd.
And in God's timing by and by,
We'll know what we should do.

So why should we be nervous,
And why should we be blue?
For God holds our tomorrows,
And in heaven there'll be no sorrow.
For if God is really for us,
Then serving Him is what we'll do.

IT'S JUST A GAME

Bowling ain't been really great
Pins fall down a little late.
Pin sweeper does the job
Of close encounters called a rob.
But I'll let these thoughts of gloom
Conquer me. I've not the room
If I should fall down on my face,
Let's hope I do it with some grace.
It's just a game , let's not forget;
It's sure not worth to throw a fit.
So if I smile despite the score,
I'll open up another door:
The door of peace and fellowship
That never comes when we just quit.

EPHESIANS

Lord, don't understand it all,
Sometimes the awful ways I fall,
Or how sometimes the circumstance
Comes against me like a trance.
Who's to blame for all these woes?
Some to Satan sure to go.
Or maybe even you could say
The Lord sent trouble down my way.
And last of all, but it could be,
The trouble really rests with me.
But as I study the Good Book
Some things require a second look;
And one of these I'd have to say
Concerns the trouble I've had today.
For in all things we are told
To give God thanks as we grow old,
In psalms and hymns and spirit life.
We're to just praise God despite the strife.
For when by faith we trust in God,
When trouble comes, it does seem odd,
We can know that even this,
Can lead us somehow into bliss.
For God's own glory and my good,
So praise the Lord, you know we should.
And when we do this in a pinch,
The Lord will bless you, it's a cinch.

Scripture basis: Ephesians 5:19-20

Speak to one another with psalms, hymns and spiritual songs.
Sing and make music in your heart to the Lord,
Always giving thanks to God the Father for everything,
In the name of our Lord Jesus Christ.

PICKING UP

"Things are picking up," he said,
The garbage man who shook his head,
And told me with a little smile.
"You know what I do is worthwhile.
My schooling didn't go too far,
But I know full well who I are.
I'm kind of simple you might think,
But with the Lord I'm in the pink.
While it's true I don't have much,
The Lord and I still keep in touch.
And these visits sure do my soul good,
Just like dear Mama taught they would."
The thought occurred as he waved goodbye,
That however smart we all will die,
And the smartest attitude in life,
Is faith in God through all the strife.
And when God's grace fills your cup,
Your life indeed starts picking up.

HOME

What kind of place do you call home?
Is it large enough that you can roam?
Or is it small beyond belief,
Just big enough to give relief?
Is your home in Snob Ridge Manor,
Where passers-by can see your banner?
Or do you live down by the tracks,
With down-and-outers, white and black?
No matter where you rest your head,
Remember as you climb into bed,
That rich or poor or in-between,
There is a God on whom to lean.
And when the Lord heads up your table,
Peace and love He will enable
To bless your home and those within,
And folks will greet you as a friend.

HE'S ALWAYS THERE

Whom am I depending on
To help me daily get along;
To do those things which must be done,
And keep on when it's just no fun?
I have a boss who signs my check
When he's not breathing down my neck.
And I've got a wife who treats me right;
We get along and seldom fight.
My preacher and a few close friends
I sometimes think that heaven sends.
And I have parents, tried and true,
Who stick beside me when I'm blue.
There're many folks who in a pinch
I'm sure will come, almost a cinch,
And every day I try my best
To pass life's challenges that test
To see what kind of man am I.
Sometimes I fail, then wonder why.
For even when supporters rally,
There's only One who adds the tally.
Did I count God as number One
And ask my questions to the Son?
Did I pray, confess my sin,
And by His Spirit start again?
I praise the Lord for human souls
Who Christ within them clearly shows.
But mostly I give thanks to God
Each day I walk upon His sod,
To know that He will always care.
When seeking Him, He's always there.

TEARS

Tears, their flowing, have a part
Which draws us closer to God's heart.
They start sometimes when we repent,
And other times it seems they're sent
When we're just on emotions high.
Sometimes we cry and wonder why.
For tears unlock our inner being;
They cleanse our eyes for better seeing.
They show our deepest needs and feelings.
Praise the Lord when He is dealing
In us with tears, no matter when
For we're exposed the greatest then.
If it's for joy our tears do flow,
Then God of love you let us know
By their own streaming down our faces
That You are real and full of graces.
And when they come when we're in pain,
Or feel alone out in the rain;
When heavy is the load we bear;
Then Lord they hasten we seek Your care.
For tears like these the Father sends,
And as they flow He also mends.
He quickens to our mind the fact
That He is real and not an act.
And only Christ can fill the gap
That fills the void in all we lack.
So tears, although not always wanted,
Often hidden, never flaunted,
Have a purpose, fill a need;
By them to God we all are keyed.
Like God's Son who also wept,
Tears can help us to connect.
For they are real, like our soul,
And humbly help to make us whole.

NO PERFECT PEOPLE

We've no perfect people here;
Not so long as I am near.
Not a one can ever claim
That they are spotless without blame.
A church can never ever be
A place completely trouble free,
For it is made of folks like us
Who fail at times and miss the bus.
We're prone to often get off center
But needing Christ our life to enter.
Every day we need renewal;
God's grace and love afresh as fuel.
For we so easy miss the mark;
Without God's love we'd lose our spark.
No perfect people, even close,
Even those who love God most.
No perfect people form Christ's church;
No point to even make a search.
Instead of looking for our faults,
Let's look to Christ whom God exalts,
To Jesus Christ who showed the way
That in God's sight we'd be OK.
Far from perfect, but just the same
There're love and healing in His name.
We see God's grace by His example,
Though we're imperfect, He is ample
To do great things with folks like us
Who need His grace and in Him trust.
Faith says that He'll do what He said;
That we're the reason Jesus bled.
For our sins He paid the fee
So by His Spirit we're set free.
Not perfect folks by any means,
But Kingdom builders He redeems.

GOD'S PROMISES

My faith is what I have right now.
The answers are not known;
I'm nothing on my own.
But Christ within me won't allow
That I give up, throw in the towel.

Hindsight says I missed some turns;
Got off the tract indeed,
In part have caused my need.
In fire now I suffer burns,
But from mistakes is how one learns.

Live for God through all the strife;
In Him will calmness be.
From chaos we will see
God's in control to bless our life.
Trust Him, husband; trust Him, wife.

It will work out and all for good.
God's promises are true;
He's here for me and you.
Pray and praise Him as we should.
Through every trouble God has stood,

There for you and there for me.
Oh, hold on tight,
Light comes to night.
When it's darkest, soon we'll see,
That God has solved our earnest plea.

CHOOSE GRACE

The grace of God I can't explain,
Nor could any man who came
From deep in sin to God's pure light,
From time of blindness now to sight.
For what we see in spirit talk
Is God's grace with us in our walk.
How can you or I pretend
To understand the grace God sends;
That for our sins He sent His Son
To pay the price for what we'd done?
While deep in sin with no remorse
God's love reached out to change our course.
We by faith can make a claim:
God's work of grace includes our name.
When we repent, pray God forgive
The awful ways we sometimes live.
When we're sincere God knows our heart,
And He'll forgive and do His part.
And when we pray Christ be our Lord
Into our soul He comes on board.
He sends His Holy Spirit near;
No more alone, we need not fear.
He compensates for what we lack,
And when we stray He calls us back.
For the grace of God knows all our faults,
But these, His chosen, He exalts.
He lifts up those who choose His grace.
One day in heaven we'll see His face.

IN GOD WE TRUST

On our money you can read
The words that more of us should heed.
"In God we trust" is clearly written.
Our predecessors thought it fitting
That these words should be printed
On all bills and in coins minted
To testify in whom we trust,
The One who formed us from the dust.
A trust in God they felt essential;
A message all of us should stencil
On the fabric of our lives.
In all our living, girls and guys,
And little children, too, must know
With trust to God we all may go.
For God is steady, and His Word is true.
The things He says you know He'll do.
And God says put your trust in Christ;
With Him we're born not once but twice.
And God says with Him peace you'll find;
Not of the world, a better kind.
We can trust God to forgive our sins.
Our troubled souls by trust He'll cleanse,
When we confess our need of Him.
Trust God, His grace will enter in.
Everyone throughout the land
Should know their lives that God has planned
To be a vessel He could use.
But trust is something that we choose.
To trust ourselves or God, our choice;
My friend I'm asking you which voice
Are you listening to today?
I pray you've chosen the better way.
Trust in God; give Him your all.
Since birth each person gets the call.
But trust calls for your faith to act
As if God's love for you is fact;
As if God's grace is what you need;
You know it is, so plant a seed.
Share your trust in God with others.
Soon in Christ you'll find new brothers.

GETTING REAL

Real heartaches, real fears
Real problems, real tears,
Not always in the mood for praise.
And yet we know we need the rays
Of God, His glory, shed on us;
We hurt so bad we'd rather cuss.
And often that's just what we do,
No better off when we are through.
For in the time of rage and fury
Only darkness seems to hurry;
Settled down, with more despair
We wonder if just one does care
And really hurt the way we do.
Could such a friend be there for you?
To hear your cry and bring relief,
The world we've found just brings more grief.
And so it is, friend, in our pain
Just as we are, to God we came
As last resort, we sought Him out
Not sure what He was all about.
And yet we knew down in our heart
That He possessed the missing part;
That God could calm the restless sea;
That He was there for even me.
So crying out, without deserving,
All used up we started serving.
We prayed by grace that God forgive.
We knew that He had life to give.
A tiny spark, some call it faith,
God put it there, in all a trace.
A spark to kindle hope inside,
God's Word was true, He never lied.
That He was with us in our trial,
Would stay right with us every mile;
That it was true, God sent His Son
Jesus Christ to be the One.
To suffer, die, and rise again,
Our sin He carried that we would win.
The spark ignited precious fuel;
Life sustaining, never cruel.
A Holy Spirit kind of flame
That speaks to us. God knows our name.
He cares for every hurt we feel.
He brings us comfort when we kneel,
In His presence if you please.
It's us who turns, He never leaves.

Precious comfort, precious care,
Precious hope, precious there.
There beside us, not far off;
We know, we know, let others scoff
No other friend, but Christ alone
Could bridge the gap, for us atone.
No other friend could pave the way
Or give us reason to obey.
Pave the way to God, His throne;
Make us worthy to be His own;
To fill our humble hearts with joy
God chose us, His girl, His boy,
To spread the Kingdom of His love,
Through us, each day, with help above.
The real heartaches, real fears,
The real problems and real tears;
God knows we can't take it alone.
That's why He wants us as His own.
For as His child we give Him trust;
And He's obliged, in fact He must
Make a way; He said He would
That all of this will work for good.
We'll have the victory when all is done
Because with Christ the victory's won.
The gloom, despair, it can't last long,
For Christ renews, gives us a song.
Restoration for our soul,
What once was broken He makes whole.
And, friend, if you don't know this joy;
You're beaten, broken, Satan's toy.
You're angry because life's not fair,
Then why not let me take you there?
You enter God's celestial gate
When enough of you, enough of hate
Puts its burden at God's feet
Admitting, Christ, we're not complete.
We don't love or serve enough;
A lump of coal, we're pretty rough.
So as we are, we come to You
Thankful this you've brought us to.
For all tomorrows that lie ahead,
World take notice, its Christ instead.
The choice we make of our free will
For real life, God's precious seal.
Have your way, Lord; mold us just right.
You are the way, the truth, and the light.

BEST OF FRIENDS

Best of friends is what we are.
Christ the Lord has led so far.
Our relationship is good;
God is molding as He should.
Best of friends, oh, what a joy!
Common ground, in God's employ.
For each of us knows Christ as Lord,
Our best friend, together moored.
Having Jesus as our friend,
Grace and love and peace a trend
Have taken over our estate.
The Holy Spirit shows we rate.
For it is quickened to our mind
God loved us when we still were blind.
Blind to know Him in His glory;
Now through us we live His story.
Not in full, but each small part
Draws us closer to God's heart.
Best of friends who are very real,
When I'm hurting pain they feel.
Best of friends, a gift of God,
Linked through Christ, our anchor rod.
Special people, best of friends,
To Christians, these are ones He sends.
For God knows clearly what we face,
So in our lives He finds a place
For special people, His own as such
To become our friends and bless us much.

GOD CAN SUPPLY

Praise God for being there for me!
Thank You, Lord, that You could see
I needed change for my own good.
You saw me through, I knew You would.
The tide had turned upon me quick;
The Devil's lies had tried their trick.
Unworthy, no good they did scream,
A nightmare, yes, and it's no dream;
And still I knew that You did care.
The world system is not fair.
You knew this, so You gave me cure;
Your Precious Son, the Christ, the Pure,
To hold onto because He proved
Our worth to God. His grace has moved
My heart to look beyond the pain
To see that growth comes from the rain.
To know that God is still in charge,
And what I need, however large,
Or however small, it doesn't matter,
God can supply off of His platter.
Why? Because He cares for me.
His vision, clear, can always see
A path to get me past the storm.
The cold world still has places warm.
And when I follow His direction,
Fixed on Christ, not my perfection,
Of which there's little to be found.
I see that things start turning around.
And this week once more it's confirmed
That even though the path has turned,
That still the God who loves my soul
Has held my hand and kept me whole.
And in ways that defy the odds
Meets my needs and He applauds.
Or so it seems, my faith He guards,
No miles of desert, only yards.
And all the time He didn't waver.
Thank you, Lord, this latest favor!

OUT OF DEBT

Getting out of debt's a chore.
Seems that all I'm working for
Never really bears the fruit;
I'm always short of enough loot.
Grand old plan to see the light;
Look ahead, the goal's in sight.
And then right out of nowhere man,
Something comes to ruin my plan.
Car blows up or sewer breaks;
I'm thankful it's not plagues of snakes.
But always world, here come the curves.
Were Job's friends right, our just deserves?
Result of sin, one way or other;
God is punishing, oh, brother.
That's the message we might hear.
Christian brothers, should we fear
The future based on Satan's lies?
It's a fact, this world tries
To find a way to steal our joy.
Don't take the bait and buy this ploy.
Christian brothers, be alert.
Recognize what's truth, what's dirt.
Problems, no one is without,
But Christ suffices, have no doubt.
It's His Spirit in our soul
That gives us peace and makes us whole.
His yoke fits us pretty well.
In His presence we can tell
That it will all work out somehow.
But right this minute we have now,
This time allotted by God's plan,
Let's use it, friend, the best we can.
And praising God and giving thanks
In God's book, it surely ranks
Close to service, prayer, and love.
Oh, precious people, look above
Beyond the problems, to the cure:
Jesus Christ, our hope, the pure.

TRUST IN THE LORD

Trust in the Lord is good advice.
It lifts the soul and is so nice
That tension somehow melts away,
And we are blessed this very day.

Trust in the Lord when things go wrong.
You will manage and a song
Will still be playing in your heart,
For God's grace covers every part.

Trust in God when you don't know
If angels fly or where they go.
For God knows all, and we do not.
He'll help us out, right on the spot.

Trust in the Lord just makes good sense
When life is howling and times are tense.
For who but God can calm the sea
And remain the same for eternity?

Trust in the Lord, the solid rock
Whose Word is true and not just talk
That came to us over years of time,
And all adds up, each verse, each line.

Trust in the Lord and do good.
Oh, not so much because we should,
But because the Lord has loved us first,
And only God can quench our thirst.

Trust in Jesus Christ today.
He'll give you peace and make a way
That He can work His love through you;
God's grace, our faith, will bring us to.

Trust in the Lord in every season,
Nail-scarred hands sufficient reason.
Trust in the Lord is the right choice.
In silent prayers God hears your voice.

Based on Proverbs 22:17-19

GOD KNOWS

A vacuum lives within each soul;
Till born again, we're just not whole.
We make the rounds of daily life,
But till we're filled, there's only strife.
Until we've reached a place at last
Where only God can heal the past,
And only God can fill the void;
Yes, nothing else, we've tried and toyed.
The bottle was a useless crutch,
And drugs and sex won't count for much.
And this whole world with all its wealth
Won't fill the void or help our health.
We need a God whom we can love.
And His assurance from above,
That though we've failed, He still cares.
And through life's trials, storms, and snares
We can press on for lights ahead,
A loving God who's made a bed,
Prepared a room where all can dwell,
Where none are sick and all are well.
Where in the Spirit we can be
In loving arms upon the knee
Of God the Father, and the Son,
And Holy Spirit all in one.
We can move on to yonder grander
If in this life we don't meander,
But set our purpose in Christ first
And love like Him through all the worst
The world may heap at your door.
You can, once you know what you're for.
You can when God has filled the gap
And taken over where you lack.
And strange and odd as it may sound,
He's been there with you all around,
Just waiting that His help you seek,
And then He comes when you are weak.
When in your fragile hour of need,
You seek Him; then your soul He'll feed.
For it is strange, but it is true,
Whatever shape, the Father knew.
For God fills up each shape of void,
When Christ His Son your heart's employed.

Struggling With God

CHANGES

We've all faced changes in our lives.
Changes come when all men strive
To keep on going and to live;
To face the problems we're faced with.
Not all these changes are for good;
There're some we'd change if we could.
And as we look back on our past,
Was there a change we'd hope would last?
There was for me, and I hope for you,
A change which really makes us new.
And that was when at last we said,
"If Lord you're real, kick my head.
Open my eyes so I can see
The love you have if it's for me."
When after years of selfish strife
I prayed "Dear Lord, enter my life."
When weak and beat down to my knees
I sought the Lord and begged Him please
To forgive my sins and enter me;
And behold was Jesus held the key.
What changed this stubborn willful man
As nothing else in this world can
Was the love of God which filled my soul
And gave me peace to make me whole.
Which came at last when I admitted
I need you Lord; now I'm committed.
A change of heart, but what a difference!
Truths hidden from me now made sense.
This change in me I hope will last.
The old life's buried in the past.

FOR WHAT IT'S WORTH

What's it worth, this life of mine?
I need to know; give me a sign.
"Do you love me, God," I ask—
"The real me, beneath the mask,
The me I mostly hide from friends?"
I know I'm not what God intends—
Not in prayer like I should be,
Mostly thinking about me.

What's it worth, this life of mine?
I wonder when will it be fine—
A life that truly shows Your beauty
Out of love instead of duty.
I struggle, Lord, and still it seems
The life I'm called to is in my dreams.
I'm not there yet; I'm still in process.
My hope rests firmly where the cross is.

What's it worth, this life of mine
That you should fill it with new wine?
The cup of life in Christ's shed blood,
His body broken, like a flood,
It hit me one day, on my knees.
Your love is grace, I cannot please,
Or by my actions ever earn
The gift your Spirit's let me learn.

For what it's worth you paid the price,
And I rejoice for what is nice.
You see in my life what can be;
Your love and grace have set me free.
And when I call on You for help,
Your Spirit comes, and it is felt.
My life worth plenty all because
You choose to shower it with love.

What's it worth, this life of mine—
Even if I'm sometime blind.
All your children, God you love,
Help us, Lord, from up above
To fully give our lives to You;
To know You better then to do,
The Kingdom building that's Your plan,
Enabling grace to reach each man.

CONFESSION

Lord, You woke me from my sleep.
You said I'm getting in too deep.
Just a little thing it seemed,
But not to Him or His redeemed.
"You are a thief!" I heard Him say.
"The thing you did was not OK."
"Go away, I need my rest!"
But He would not, and that was best.
Up and pacing on the floor,
Why, oh why, did I ignore
The truth I knew right from the first?
Correct it now; avoid the worst.
Get it settled and make amends.
God rebukes the time He sends
Words like these which pierce my soul.
He's calling me, "I want you whole."
Close to Christ, the sin must go.
I'm making sure that you know
Your actions really weren't in line
With what's expected from one of mine
Miserable. That's how I felt.
A payback for the card I'd dealt.
I knew the next day I must face
The one I'd wronged and hope for grace.
I must confess and set things straight.
The time is now. It cannot wait.
Not an easy thing to do,
But with God's help He'd see me through.
And so He did, and I'll sleep better.
My debt of sin cleaned off the ledger.
Confessing what God showed was sin
Has brought deep peace to me within.

GOD'S MATH

I have failed on many counts.
My brain's not using every ounce
Of knowledge locked somewhere inside.
In pity parties I have cried:
"Not really fair; oh, look at them,
A future bright, but mine seems dim."
And so it goes, the accusations—
You've no worth, it seems a mission;
Satan playing with my mind.
Who needs the garbage of this kind?
Honest labor, job well done,
All peace I've know is in the Son.
Jesus lover of my soul;
He's the reason I'm made whole.
It's not the balance in the bank
That holds the key to how I rank
In the eyes of Lord Creator.
No, there's something even greater
To the Lord who owns it all,
Who made provision for my fall.
Did I confess and repent of sin,
And ask Christ Jesus enter in
To the depth of who I am;
To be in Him all that I can,
A vessel seeking out the Spirit,
Taking time to find and hear it;
All this goes against the flow,
The world says we ought to know.
Sure-fire ways to strike it rich,
And comforts there for every itch.
And if your neighbor makes the grade,
Perhaps your car you better trade.
A worldly picture out of whack,
But let me share with you a fact
That I have learned along life's path.
It has to do with Godly math.
True joy in life comes when we serve,
And peace abides to calm the nerve.
For every step towards God we take,
There're ten towards us the Lord will make.

GOD'S SPIRIT IS LOVING PROOF

What will people think?
What will people say?
Born again but now you drink.
Was it real or only play?

You love the Lord,
And you feel His call,
But now you're bored.
What made you fall?

A holy life is ideal.
We honor those who act that way.
Such persons hold a strong appeal;
Firmly grounded they seldom sway.

Such fine folks are rare indeed.
They are the salt of the earth.
More of them we surely need.
More of us need rebirth.

I am one who's felt God's love,
And with the Lord I've been blessed.
But not all thoughts are from above;
And as a Christian I'd flunk a test.

Thank God for grace sufficient,
To forgive and love me though I goof.
For when I pray and repent,
I feel His Spirit as loving proof.

I know I can never earn God's love.
Thank God He loves me though I fail.
But with your Spirit from above
I'll try to stay close on your trail.

MILDLY DISTURBED

Mildly disturbed is what I am.
I'm not doing all I know I can.
And yet the things I've done for good,
Don't work out how I thought they would
When helping others, I would think
That help would somehow be a link
To gain approval and respect,
And not be judged as some defect.
But many times we do our best
And really try to pass the test,
To be there when it really counts,
And catch the ball on the first bounce.
And then when we ask small return,
Like courtesy and thanks I learn,
That these are often cast aside,
And in your need these people hide.
Not all people act this way,
Least often those who love and pray.
But when the ones we love the most
Reject us, well it comes real close,
To casting doubt on our sad minds,
That Jesus is the tie that binds.
But if your faith in Christ is rooted,
You'll soon discover you're not suited
To hold onto these thorny barbs,
For Christ has made your heart too large,
And you would sooner forgive and let
Some other fish fall into the net,
That Satan set to steal your joy.
An ancient trick he did employ.
Yes, mildly I am disturbed,
For I sometimes heed this blurb.
But when I think how Christ did suffer,
For sins of mine it helps to buffer
These pangs of grief for minor wrongs
And reminds me where my soul belongs.
For I'm not here just to be blessed,
And until I'm dead I'm not to rest;
And say, "Well, Lord, I've done enough.
This helping others is too rough."
For when the time comes that we're done,
And we say we'll help just when it's fun,
God's light will fade away from us,
And we might just miss heaven's bus.
Disturbed at times is only normal,
But clothed in it's an awful formal.
Put on the robe of Christian love,
And God will help you from above.
To overcome these earthly snares,
God knows all and really cares.

MONDAY EVENING

Monday evening all alone,
It's quiet here without a phone.
My kids I love beyond measure.
They're part of me, my greatest treasure.
Why, oh Lord, is things this way?
Will things ever again be OK?
The road ahead is not mine to see.
With faith in God my soul's set free.
No, I'm not happy with this deal,
But does faith come from what we feel?
If this were so, we'd all be doomed.
I think on all the times I've fumed.
The Lord is always true to His Word.
If He's lied once, I've never heard.
Retaliate to settle the score;
Is this what God made us for?
It's not according to the Book I read.
Thoughts like these old Satan breeds.
No, we're supposed to follow Christ's example.
Forgive the ones who on our lives did trample.
Pray for the ones who are lost in sin,
And pray for ourselves when we begin.
For if we can't find forgiveness of others,
Christ cannot count us as one of His brothers.
The situation may not be pleasant,
But in all things the Lord can be present.
God is never from our lives off far,
But it may seem that way from where we are.
When we lose faith and see just the external,
We jeopardize now and perhaps the eternal.
Trust the Lord and follow His Word;
Your spirit will soar like the flight of a bird.
Contemplate on how much God loves you;
You're bound to feel better and less blue.
Yes, Monday evening, I'm all alone,
But because God loves me I'll not groan.
I pray, dear Lord, your will be done.
Be with my family, yes, everyone.

HOLY SPIRIT, DON'T LEAVE ME NOW

Don't leave me now, Holy Spirit.
What's right with me you helped form.
This force of God, by grace, I cheer it.
It's helped me past the greatest storm.

In times of reverence You are here.
While seeking God in humble prayer,
Just how you come is not always clear.
It's more a feeling of precious care.

I don't deserve this heavenly gift.
I've been rebellious most of my life,
But a deep need inside needed a lift.
It could not be supplied by man or wife.

Only God could provide what I needed.
The peace and the joy and the love only came,
When Jesus took root from faith slowly seeded.
Holy Spirit lives when it's Jesus we claim.

But sometimes my life gets off the track,
And unholy thoughts lead me far away.
When I think I've arrived, the devil attacks,
And I wonder, Lord, why did I sway.

Was it for enjoyment I let You down,
Or were earthly pressures my poor excuse?
Without Your hand, I'd quickly drown,
And for Your Kingdom I'd be of no use.

So what's the reason I should try
To live a life that God would approve,
When basically I'm a sinful guy
And odds are such that I should lose?

The reason lies at Calvary's cross.
That for my sins Christ died for me.
The Lord, in grace, doesn't want me lost,
But wants me clean and fit for Thee.

And the Holy Spirit leads the way
To help me with the spiritual battles.
And though I may fail on certain days,
A prayer for forgiveness the world rattles.

For in returning to the source of our strength,
Which is none other than Christ Jesus,
Our fullness of life is not measured in length,
But rather in service to Him who frees us.

LOWER NATURE

I have a lower nature.
God how I know it!
In some ways a strange creature;
Love God but cause Him a fit.
I'm blessed to be a blessing to others.
Material things don't cause much joy.
Serving Christ is winning the soul of a brother.
It's an honor to bring the gospel to each girl and boy.
But, Lord, I've not given You every part of my being.
Deep down I enjoy my lustful evils.
Shame on me because I know you're seeing.
I'm like the chicken attacked by the weevils.
I thank You, Lord, for the victories given.
Faith has cast off most of the rot.
I need You, Lord, in all areas of my living.
I want more, Lord, of what You've got.
You love me, Lord, of this I'm sure.
Let me use Your shield of faith
To stop Satan's fiery darts that makes me impure.
I pray, Dear Lord, I'm still in Your grace.

TRYING TIMES

Times like this try my soul,
Just how much, oh God, you know.
To walk this earth and know you care,
Is my only salvation from complete despair.
My wife and kids are turned against me.
What's good within me they can't see.
Holy Spirit, please touch my wife.
She's oh, so lost and needs new life.
I love my family but can't take anymore.
To live in pain we're not made for.
Lord, I pray You'll understand my plight;
Your Spirit's on me - give me flight.
To my wife I've witnessed as I must.
She won't see. Shall I shake the dust?
Things about me I know are wrong,
But to see only these just kills my song.
So, Lord, forgive me if I'm wrong,
But I'm in a marriage I don't belong.
Help me, Lord, to escape from grief.
Only You can save me is my belief.

OUT OF WORK

I feel like I'm all washed up,
Unwanted and I'm out of luck.
My confidence is running low,
A trick of Satan, yes, I know.
I'm old, not really, but I feel
Disappointed with this deal.
Seems I try to do my best
But somehow fail to pass the test.
What's wrong with me anyhow?
Moods like this I can't allow,
To rob my peace and give me grief.
Jesus, give me some relief
From how I feel. It serves no good.
Things will work out as they should.
If I can keep my faith intact,
God will supply all that I lack.
Confidence, it comes from Him.
Help me, Lord, to try and grin.
Odds I know are stacked against me;
But something right, I must agree
Is out there, Lord, help me connect.
It will be good I do expect.
These days are rough; they try my soul,
But Lord you're good; You make me whole.

DON'T GIVE UP

You've lived a time without a faith
And almost were a basket case.
Thank God you saw the light;
The love of Jesus cleared your sight.
You knew you were a child of God,
And friends thought you were acting odd.
The love you felt so deep inside
Was from God and not to hide.
But mountain tops don't last forever,
And Satan's storms brought gloomy weather.
The world tries to knock you down
And change that smile to a frown.
Those who've never met the Lord
Bring on havoc with their sword.
Do not listen to such chatter;
Trust the Lord with every matter.
The Lord is there when you ask;
He's there to help you with each task.
Though the outlook doesn't look good,
Pray to God as you know you should.
God will never leave you stranded,
If joined with Him your love is banded.
So my advice is to not give up.
Let the love of God fill your cup.

DRUM TEMPER

One moment at peace with the Savior,
The next moment's strife, not in anyone's favor.
I'm having trouble figuring it out.
What makes me so prone to shout?

I can pray and feel close to heaven,
And I can erupt before the count of seven.
Most times I'm quiet and calm,
Sweetness and light as morning dawn.

I love God above all else
Because He loves me more than myself.
So, Lord, why do I have a quick temper?
Sad if that about me is what folks remember.

It's a part of my make up I'd best be without.
Lord, can you steer me on a better route?
Guilt I'm feeling is the Spirit scolding.
Does this mean with me You are still molding?

Not dead and room to improve...
Help, Lord, it's our move.
I'm not ready, Lord, to stand on the scale,
And I know it's Your desire that none should fail.

Lord, I pray You will help with this problem.
It will help me serve better and beat your drum.

DISCONTENT

With how things are I'm not contented.
I've served you, Lord, and have repented.
So what's the reason I'm still shook up?
I've sought your guidance and read your book.
I know, dear Lord, you are forgiving,
But I need more for where I'm living.
A deeper faith to place my trust;
There is growth in valleys but not in lust.
I've grown in sorrow but have not reached
That closeness of God the preachers preach.
Oh, I can pray and feel God near,
But God is not the only voice I hear.
"Poor me" is a tune which is repeated.
I've felt, dear Lord, I've been mistreated.
And the ones whose love I've most sought after
Have left me now and stolen my laughter.
Perhaps, dear Lord, you'll hear my plea:
To rest in You and be set free.
Help me, Lord, to walk in your Spirit.
Your still soft voice, I long to hear it.
I'm bored with simply being good.
Please mold and shape me as you should.

GOD'S SOLUTION

Problems sure have come my way
Both yesterday and now today.
And if I live another week,
The problems may be twice as steep.
It seems in life you can be sure
That many times you must endure
A struggle that may seem unfair,
Then wonder does the Savior care.
The prayer you prayed that wasn't met—
The way you thought, at least not yet.
The friend who failed in your need
Concerned with self and full of greed.
The human folly, that's our lot.
It's just the reason we should not
Forsake the One who loves our souls,
And wants His peace to make us whole.
For problems we will have each day;
But only Christ can show the way
That we can live life to the full,
And feel God's present gentle pull.
To give Him thanks His grace exceeds
More fully than to meet our needs.
For problems are a way God chose
To keep us mindful that He knows
The situation and the plan
And wants our faith; all that we can,
To keep our purpose stayed in Him.
That's when solutions can begin.

TELL GOD YOUR FRUSTRATIONS

Expressing ourselves sometimes means
Frustration's mangled hopes and dreams
Are hung outside for all to see.
The real person known as me,
Lets it fly, the inner self;
Discontent spills off the shelf.
And when the geyser's had its flow
I'll back away, my head hung low,
And say I'm sorry I spouted off,
And hideaway into my loft.
And then when I have settled down,
Sometimes I'll kneel to the ground,
And ask that God once more forgive
The selfishness in how I live.
I'll ask that God would oversee
The fears and problems known to me,
And teach me how to rest in Him.
God's Holy Spirit helps me then.
For if we'll seek, then we will find
Our loving Father who's always kind.

LAMENT

This circumstance has me blue;
It seems there's more that I should do.
This is a time my family's divided;
The ones I loved have left me chided.
I'm working hard with little to show,
And the wife and kids suffer, I know.
So why do I bother to keep going?
The more that I try the problems keep growing.
Sometimes I think I'll go and get drunk,
But that would just help me to smell like a skunk.
I'm frustrated and bothered with no place to go,
But to those all around me I put on a good show.
Yes, all you people, I do love the Lord.
His love within me has strengthened my cord,
But my strength is not what I'm worried about.
It's my kids now, not with me, doing without.
Lord I pray my kids will return.
Living together in love may we learn.
And Lord I pray for my wife who is lost.
The results of separation have sure had its cost.
And, Lord, how I know I'm far from the mark;
Although I still love you, where goes my spark?
Lord, please help me over this slump.
Help me get my kids out of that dump.
And, Lord, if you give the help that I seek,
I'll love you and praise you week after week.

FLICKER FAITH

Sometimes our faith is mighty weak;
It's hard to pray; it's hard to seek.
We feel we should take a break;
God grant us rest for heaven sake.
There's only so much we can do,
So much, dear Lord, is up to You.
We get discouraged often times
By constant paying of our fines.
The things we said we shouldn't have;
The wounds we caused now needing salve.
Our purpose somehow not so clear
We wonder, Lord, are you still near.
We thought one time we knew the light;
That with Christ Jesus all was right.
That never more would we know sorrow,
That only good could come tomorrow.
Flicker faith at times so dim,
Just on occasion do thoughts of Him
Really stir our sleepy soul;
More times we're not completely whole.
What's the problem? Why the fuss?
Perhaps our focus looks at us.
Looks at you and looks at me,
Gets disappointed with what we see.
And we lose sight of God's sweet grace,
Forget Christ died to take our place.
We think that we should somehow earn
God's precious love, in fact we spurn.
We get ourselves right in the way,
Not letting loose to God each day.
A flicker faith which knows God's light;
My friend we need it burning bright.
Oh sure, the candle does OK,
But it can sure be blown away.
We need God's light bright as the sun,
So put Him first and count it done.
The price was paid to set us free.
Let's praise Him now on bended knee.

TIME WITH GOD

Not close enough have I been;
Not close enough to stop all sin.
Not close enough to my sweet Lord,
Despite the fact He is the cord.
My strength and anchor in life's swell;
Through troubled storms I sure could tell.
My faith in God did ease the pain,
And I could smile while in the rain.
But even so with all He's done,
Myself I list as number one
To solve the problems in my path.
I'm sure it gives my Lord a laugh.
But if you're honest with yourself,
Don't we all pass up the wealth
Of God's direction in our life
When we give Him a stingy slice
Of time with Him in meditation?
More prayer is needed in our nation.
Thus said, it hinges first with me
To rectify the faults I see.
For basically it comes right down
To the fact with God I stay around
As much or little as I seek;
Sometimes just minutes in a week.
We're as close to God as we want to be,
And if I'm far away the fault's with me.

LIMITS

It's so strange
Feel the change
The current fixture
What a mixture

Rules laid down
Cause a frown.
Can light show?
I don't know.

Trust and obey,
No other way—
What's it mean?
Lord I've seen

Work You've done
With this one
To carry a torch
To all sorts.

Now facing limits
At my whit's
What's gone wrong?
Where's the song?

What's the reason
For this season?
I don't know.
Lord, please show

What you're doing.
Looks like ruin—
Could it be?
I ask of Thee.

You've taken over
Fields of clover,
In Your hands
All my plans.

Need more trust.
Lord You must
Make it clear
I need not fear.

You will prevail.
God cannot fail.
Thy will be done.
Praise God, the Son!

And Holy Spirit
How I cheer it!
Grace wins out
There's no doubt.

This will pass
And at last,
Your sweet Spirit
I will hear it.

Feel Your love
From up above—
So binding together
People we treasure.

Christ the source
Will, of course,
Tend His own
In ways shown.

That limit limits.
He still fits
In our need.
Faith a seed

Will endure.
Behold the cure.
Christ is Lord!
Christ is Lord!

BABES IN CHRIST

God loves His babies be they small
Or born again and six feet tall.
Special grace God holds for these,
Babies call them if you please.
Some are ten and some eleven.
Some are old, just short of heaven.
And many in their middle years
Have found the Lord who dried their tears.
And now, not being quite mature,
God's love they question, not so sure.
Slips and falls and doubts recurring,
The world, its hold, is still alluring.
Saved, yes but, no way snapped perfect;
Failures, feeling like a reject.
Questions babes in Christ explore,
Is it true Christ is the door?
A purpose-centered Godly life,
Not yet achieved, there's still such strife.
But praise the Lord, He saw our need!
The greatest faith was once a seed
Planted somewhere down the line.
Grace of God, it takes some time,
And prayer and study of the Word
To penetrate it must be heard.
Babies we may be for years,
Each time sought, God calms our fears.
Even when we're sliding back,
And Satan presses, full attack,
God's Holy Spirit calls His own.
Babes are born, but they're not grown
Overnight and fully rooted;
Milk suffices till they're suited.
Till they're doers of the Word,
And share the gospel truth they've heard
And put some action with their talk.
Babes mature as they walk the walk.
Letting God's light shine through them,
Winning battles over sin.
But, friend, no matter whom we are,
A babe in Christ or one gone far,
We need the Savior God has planned
In all life's journey, hand in hand.

PEACE WITH GOD

My God has never let me down;
I've felt His presence all around.
There're ones I've loved who've disappointed;
More of God's love I need anointed.
The Lord's led me to mountain tops,
And I've felt Him near while on the rocks.
I need God's grace now more than ever;
By faith in God I'm held together.
There is in store a far better day;
The Lord I know will show the way.
The love and peace and joy I've felt,
Is when God's Spirit with me has dealt.
And in these times of deepest gloom,
God will meet me in my darkened room.
While on my knees in reverent prayer,
I know, dear Lord, you really care.
Yes, people disappoint and hurt,
And the world may put me in the dirt.
My goals and dreams seem almost shattered,
But for my sins Christ's blood was splattered.
When this cruel world fills my head with doubt,
I look to the cross to see what God's love is about.
And though the storm rages all around,
With you, dear Lord, peace and joy are found.

IN HIS IMAGE

In His image God gave life to both of us.
Loved of God, He seeks our trust.
"Please seek My will in your lives,"
God calls to husbands and wives.
Aware before we ask of all our needs,
Seek the Lord first the Bible reads.
God will answer that honest prayer;
Our hands in His, no better care.
Not our wills, but yours, Lord;
We fail by ourselves, see the record.
Without God we are trash;
Ones we love we mash.
Cold of heart we lie,
Destroying and hurting by and by.
Eye of darkness causes much pain.
Selfishness brings only rain.
With faith just in ourselves, we are the fool.
With faith in God to use us, we are His tool.
Open to His Spirit, love inside is growing;
Jesus the example, it's God we're knowing.
When this great love goes from head to heart,
We're born again, new life, a new start.
In Jesus' name, Devil off our backs;
Supply us the strength Lord that we lack.
Give us a right spirit we pray.
Lost without you, Lord, there's no other way.
We're evil by nature, God show us the way.
Help us understand what your Word does say.
Help us love one another
And treat others as a brother.
Help us love and respect the one we married,
And be good parents to the kids we've carried.
You are the potter, Lord; we are the clay.
Mold us to be better; please start today.
Lord, please fill us with your grace;
Your light in us, let it show on our faces
Please forgive us for our many wrongs.
In God our faith belongs.
Within me I feel God's love flowing.
Next time, maybe, I'll write a better poem.

CHRISTIAN LIFE

Let us learn to be more kind.
Help us, Lord, to have your mind.
That is to say we want to be,
By grace a vessel fit for Thee.
Forgive us, Lord, that we have failed,
Though for our sins your Son was nailed
To Calvary's cross on Golgotha hill;
For me His precious blood did spill.
We've failed Lord; at times we're weak.
More of your Spirit we should seek.
To be like Jesus I believe
Is how you're wanting us to please.
For when we're putting others first,
We're satisfying Jesus' thirst.
And when we feed a fellow man,
We're living according to Your plan.
And if in anger we attack,
By grace, through prayer, You'll take us back.
Moment by moment it seems we're tested;
How long with Jesus till fully vested?
The answer, my friend, is clear as day:
Always, forever, He is the Way!
You'll never outgrow your need for Him.
Without His Spirit your light will dim.
You cannot be a shining light,
If He's not with you day and night.
And if you'll not take time to pray;
To love His Word and to obey,
Then you will quickly soon discover
You've lost your best friend and your brother.
But He's not the one who's left your side.
It's you who wants to run and hide.
"Take up my cross" you've heard Him say.
The burden's there, but that's the way.
No easy walk this Christian life,
But inward peace will calm the strife.
And you will know beyond a doubt,
His love's the kind you can't live without.

LONELY

It's Friday evening: I'm alone.
Last place I want to see is home.
For my small shanty grows on me.
Freedom's not all it's supposed to be,
Just empty space devoid of love.
I pray for peace from God above.
Can't understand the plight I'm in.
Keep trying but seems I never win.
I tried to please my kids and wife,
Then they just walked out of my life.
I forgave a friend for shameful deeds,
But constant lying marks the life he leads.
I feel like I've just been used.
Lord mend my spirit lest I be bruised.
Self pity is the Devil's trick.
Moods like this I wouldn't pick.
But this is the way I feel just now,
And I'm in no mood to kneel and bow.
I need to escape from this lament;
It's time that could sure be better spent.
But still I shy away from crowds.
Don't like it where it's way too loud.
Still needing time to be alone,
But, damn, I wish my kids would phone!
I wish my home could someday be
A place where all have love for Thee.
A place where Jesus' name is spoken,
Filled with loving, gentle folk and,
For this sweet vision to come true,
Lord, please in-fill me fresh and new.
Lord, help my spirit to revive;
I need your blessing to survive.
And, Lord, I pray more than that,
 You'll help me move from where I'm at.

JAIL

Here in jail is sure no fun.
It's crossed my mind that I should run.
But I've a debt which must be paid.
This bed of thorns is what I made.
I know that this won't last forever,
And when I'm out I sure will never
Repeat those things which put me here;
I'd just assume get nowhere near.
Now, Lord, I think it's time we met.
I've been as far away as I can get.
And, Lord, I know you've seen my sin
And all the awful things within.
So I just ask in humble prayer,
Forgive my sins and show you care.
For, Lord, I admit that I am weak;
When tempted I sure want to peek.
It's hard for me to stay on line,
And it hurts to have to pay the fine.
So, Lord, at last in this life's juncture,
I pray dear, Lord, this life you'll puncture;
And let me learn to lean on you
And feel your Spirit through and through.
I need your light to lead the way.
I think it's time that I obey.
So, Lord, if you will meet me here,
My eyes may shed a little tear,
For I am ready for your touch.
Unworthy, yet I need you much.

PARDON ME

Lord, I'm begging, would you please
Hear my prayer, I'm on my knees.
I've sinned against you, this I know
And now I'm feeling pretty low.
My shame, my guilt, you know it well.
No doubt about it; I surely fell.
My prayer, dear Lord, is simply this:
That you would pardon the whole list
Of all the sins I'm guilty of
And put into me more of your love.
The gift of life you've blessed me with,
I've botched not knowing how to live.
So now by faith I plead the blood,
Repenting from a life of crud.
I see the error of my ways.
My life of darkness needs the rays
Of life, of hope, of joy, of peace;
The light of Jesus' sweet release.
I've had the world, and it's had me;
So precious Lord please set me free.
These chains of sin I give to You.
By faith in Christ I am made new.
And even as I'm praying now,
I feel Your Spirit with me somehow.
My slate is clean from this time on.
I'm pardoned though I've been all wrong.
The joy I'm feeling in my soul
Is there because You've made me whole.
It's hallelujah shouting ground.
Oh, Lord, I'm thankful You've been found!
And while other pardons from men I seek,
Your grace and love will let me sleep.
For all my life and problems, too, -
By faith, dear Lord, I trust to You.

REVIVAL

Alive in Christ we should celebrate;
Lord, help us live to show this trait.
Life is tough and can be a grind;
Lord help us always to be kind.
There are ones we've loved who have moved along;
Lord, comfort our hurt and give us a song.
Too busy with living to study God's Word;
Lord, lead us in ways that your Word is heard.
Finances are hurting, can hardly pay taxes;
Lord, let us not cheat you, your spirit backs us.
So many problems causes our faith to wane;
Lord, fill us with your love: make it abundantly plain.
Closed doors in our faces, can we face what's next?
Lord strengthen our spirit; You wrote the text.
We let circumstances sometimes steal our joy;
Lord remind us again that we're your girl or boy.
Regardless of age from the time we are saved,
Lord, help us grow strong and in your Spirit be bathed.
Living waters will flow when our spirit's revived.
Lord, revive me; I'm low because I've dived.
I've not made Jesus my best friend in the world.
Lord, fill me inside, in your spirit be curled.
Revival indeed, yes, daily we need it;
Lord, now at this time let us get lit.
A light to the world is what you place inside;
Lord, revive us again so your light we'll not hide.
In sweet abandon let us be used just for you;
Lord, revive us now so to you we'll be true.
Revivals ahead. Let's pray to be ready.
Lord, praise your name and help us stay steady.
By His stripes we are healed so the scripture reads.
Lord show us now you're all that we need.
Not existing, but living in the best sense of the word;
Lord speak to our hearts, revive and be heard.

ONE DAY I'LL SEE YOUR FACE

Problems that I'm facing now
Will all work out, I pray somehow.
I think perhaps we're not to know
The final sequence of the show.
Instead we're supposed to live on faith;
God's precious time we're not to waste.
For we have nothing apart from God,
His love and strength our anchor rod.
Our shoulders can't bear all the weight
Of an evil world that's full of hate.
The world demands that we take part
And join the crowds that push and shove,
Forgetting acts of Christian love.
So, Lord, I pray you'll hold me firm.
Don't let me catch old Satan's germ,
And keep me humbly at Your call.
Without Your light I've none at all.
And I'll praise you daily for your grace;
One day in heaven I'll see your face.

CLAIM THE THRONE

Without the rain upon my brow,
Without the rain I doubt somehow
That I could ever fully see
The love my Savior has for me.
For when your life's turned upside down,
And friends you need just can't be found;
It's in the moments such as these,
We pray in earnest God just please,
Take this yoke off my back,
And fill me Lord just where I lack.
For until we pray with reverent zeal,
We're not prepared God's love to feel.
But we needn't wait for rainy days
To seek the Lord and give Him praise.
He's waiting for you every day
To show Himself and lead the way.
And when you daily claim the throne,
His loving Spirit will become your own.

REPENTANT SINNERS HEART

Lord, help me to forget and forgive
Sins directed at me in deceit.
I have my own faults;
Please forgive my trespasses and doubts.
Lord, please remove the want to sin;
Lord, draw me closer to your skin.
I have been wrong most of the time.
Please help me escape from this slime.
The mark of a Christian is a loving heart.
You may quote scripture and to others seem smart.
But entering heaven on the judgment day
Isn't dependent on what others say.
The Lord God almighty will put our lives on a scale.
How we live now determines if we pass or fail.
The time to forgive and get right is now.
Don't wait, farmer, for that field to plow.
Change now before your heart gets too cold.
Let God hold you and have something to mold.
For none of us is perfect;
We've sinned and been low as a serpent.
Who but Christ can save us?
Thank you, Lord, for abundant grace.
Thank you, Lord, for showing your face.
Thank you, Lord, for the love you place
Into a repentant sinner's heart, as in my case.

DEPENDENCE ON GOD

Thank you, Lord, for giving me life.
Pardon me, Lord, for causing such strife.
Wanting to serve you is my plan.
Dying out to self is toughest part.
First, love the Lord as much as I can.
Trusting God's a good place to start.
Lord, why do I tend to look at the problems,
Prince of darkness, favorite goblins?
Faith gives hope causing light to shine.
Admitting dependence on God is a big step.
I love you, Lord, and you are mine.
If surrounded in His love we are kept.
To have a Christian home is my prayer,
A home of love that is there.
This is not an impossible dream.
We must love each other more than self,
And love and trust God more than anything.
Our family will be blessed beyond any wealth.

I NEED GOD EVERY HOUR

Lord, I need You right this hour.
I need your love and grace and power.
In fact I need You all the time;
Each moment with You is so fine.
I'm thankful last week in a stew
You showed me quickly what to do.
And many, many other times
You helped me bravely cross those lines.
And I am richer now today
Because your light has shown the way.
And now today, unlike the past,
I see You first instead of last,
And pray the knowledge You are near
Will help me overcome my fear;
And do what's pleasing in your sight
Throughout this day into the night.

BLUNDER MAN

Lord I have to sometimes wonder
What's the reason I still blunder?
If to screw up were your great plan,
In me, dear Lord, you've found your man.
My finances now lie in shambles;
My home resembles thorns and brambles.
The ones I loved have moved away;
About me they've no good to say.
I'm lucky if I can keep my job;
I'm dumb sometimes as a log.
So let me ask another question:
Are you trying to teach me a lesson?
Perfect I'm not is plain as day;
In truth I think I'm made this way.
Mistakes and all I still feel your love.
Your Spirit's with me, not just above.
I thank you, Lord, for joy you've brought
To a fool like me who's not been taught,
To live a life free of all error,
But to love you, Lord, and be a care-er.
I'll try my best to do your will;
To succeed at this would be a thrill.
I pray your Spirit with me won't leave,
For this by faith I do believe.
That though I often make mistakes,
You will supply all that it takes
To lead my life in your direction,
A humble life but not perfection.

39TH BIRTHDAY

Lord, you have blessed me with 39 years.
Your love for me has calmed my fears.
At the present my family is lost;
Following You Lord has had its cost.
All things considered it may be my fault.
Are there ways of my being you're wanting to halt?
I am nothing with no reason to brag.
Compared to Your glories, I'm a sleaze bag.
And though I know I'm unworthy as dust
I know you made me, so in You I'll trust.
The world I've learned can be so unfair;
It's good to know Lord You still care.
Since I've come to You, Lord, I've been able to sing,
While those that I love try to take everything.
I guess now is the time to try and be brave,
For what's right within me, I'd like to save.
The only part of me that has any worth
Is the part that you hold that's given new birth.
I know You're the reason, Lord, for all that is good.
I've not given You all the praise that I should.
My mind can hardly take it all in,
But what I know of You, Lord, can make me grin.
My smile comes because I've felt Your love;
You're not on some cloud just drifting above.
And though I'm not worthy in action or deed,
You've come as my helper in greatest need.
I often fail and get spiritually off center.
It's by grace and forgiveness Your presence re-enters.
Thank You, Lord, for the avenue of prayer.
You will hear a prayer from anywhere.
You know best, Lord, what my prayer should be.
More of You, Lord, is what I want in me.
In 39 years I'll be seventy eight.
With You in my life, Lord, I commend my fate.

THE PIT

If we were stuck down in a hole
Without another human soul
To know the pit that we fell into,
Do you suppose that even then,
If we could pray a silent prayer,
Our God would answer with His care?
If it were hopeless in our view
Could God supply, afresh and new
The reassurance of His love
And give us help from above?
It may seem useless, what the heck,
But does not faith, the smallest speck
Begin when we, complete at loss
Take our problem to the cross
And say, dear God, I've reached the end;
Enough of me, Lord would you send
A comfort in my hour of need.
Your Holy Spirit, let it feed
This life, disrupted to the core
And show me, Lord, the life, the door.
Well, friend, I've been down in that pit,
Was dying and about to quit
When I decided, last resort
To pray in earnest, center court
And ask that God, by grace alone
Would let His light to me be shown.
And shine, He did, I'll have you know;
My Jesus reached me when down low.
The debt of love to God I feel
Is in my soul, I know it's real.
So I must do what God commands,
Just love Him first, then grab the hands
Of people reaching out in need
And give them help and plant a seed
That they are likewise in God's view
A precious person God wants to
Draw into fellowship with Him.
He's waiting first that you begin.

GRACE

Lately haven't done much good
To spread God's Kingdom like I should.
Instead been busy with some chores,
The leaking roof, the sticking doors.
I've gone to bed just plumb worn out,
My spirits has seen a little drought.
The time I set aside for prayer
Has lately been a little rare.
For life is pressing in on me;
The clock is ticking, can't you see?
And I have things which must be done,
And roofing's one which sure ain't fun.
So, Lord, I ask would you forgive
Me for the way I sometimes live
And give to you a tiny part
Of what I have? It isn't smart.
But, Lord, deep down, within my heart
I offer You a special part.
A part that's thankful for each day
And all the blessings sent my way.
A knowledge etched upon my soul
That by Your Spirit I am whole.
For You love me; yes, even when
I'm not as close as I had been.
I know it's not my right as such,
But just Your grace I need so much.

PRAYER FOR HEALING

Lord, I'm aching in my back:
I'm not faking, I'm set back.
It hurts to move around at all;
So much to prove, I still can crawl.
I still can get down on my knees.
Before I quit, I'll ask you please
If in Your wisdom You find best
That by Your Son I might find rest.
My body needs a healing touch;
It's not by deeds I ask for such.
I only pray You'll make me well
So that I may proceed to tell
As many folks as I can find
You're not a hoax just in my mind.
But You are real, a sovereign God
Whose love I feel despite all odds.
My faith tells me You're working now;
I need not see or dare ask how.
I just believe Your Word is true,
Now I receive the love of You.

TODAY'S PRAYER

This day, Lord, your will I pray.
Give me strength, Lord, to obey
And be the vessel You can use.
Use me, Lord, the way You choose.
And by Your Spirit let me be
A vessel Lord that's fit for Thee.
I pray, dear Lord, You'll take my hand
And keep me close, Lord, as you planned.
For, Lord, without Your Spirit near,
The world, its problems, causes fear.
But when I call on Christ Your Son
Your Spirit shows me I'm the one
Who caused a sacrifice be made;
My sins forgiven Jesus paid.
So, Lord, I ask what can I do
To spread Your Kingdom? Lord renew.
And let the story of Your grace
Clearly show upon my face
So when I see a soul in need,
Concern will translate into deed.
And, Lord, my Father, may You glory
As Christ with me tells the story.

FELLOWSHIP WITH GOD

Gosh, it's great to breathe God's air,
A comfort just to be aware
That God Almighty, Prince of Grace
Knows exactly what I face.
And He has promised good to me
If by His Spirit I'll not flee.
My Lord has come up with a plan
That you and I and every man
May walk in fellowship with God
Just like the prophets we applaud.
We can be holy if we stand
Beside the Master, hand in hand.
We do this very sort of thing
Each time we pray to Christ and bring
Our problems, worries, and our praise,
To God in prayer all of our days.

THOUGHTS ON PRAYER

Praying often times involves
Things the Holy Spirit solves.
Things that only God can handle;
Go to Him for He can tell
Exactly what you need right now.
He'll make a way and show you how,
That you can live from day to day,
Empowered by Him all the way
To let your faith in Christ His Son
Join with you so two as one
Can make the choice that's really right;
To back off some or stay and fight.
To give you strength when you're defeated,
A helping hand says it's completed.
God's in charge, and He knows best;
Do what you can, give Him the rest.
But do in ways that God approves.
That's why the Bible is good news.
Pray that God reveals His truth;
Those now bound that He would lose.
That sins that you and I commit,
That He'd forgive and we would quit.
When we're sincere, God knows we are,
And His Holy Spirit isn't far.
The Spirit shows us how to pray;
It turns the darkness into day.
Our burdens will not seem so grim
The more we share and give to Him.
And when we praise God as we pray
An extra blessing comes our way.
For we will find the peace He brings
That comes our way on angels' wings
To calm the storm and bring relief.
God answers prayers is my belief.

COURT DAY

Lord, tomorrow help me be
At peace with you so I can see
That you are still in full control.
Lord, help me still to feel your pull,
And know beyond the slightest doubt
That you are with me all about.
No matter what the world may say,
I know You are the truth, the way.
Just let me put my trust in You;
To know that You will pull me through.

COMPASSION

Compassion is the sort of word
That evokes memories when it's heard.
We think about those certain folks,
That even when pressed to the ropes,
Still stood up for what was right;
We're pleased to keep up the good fight.
For their beliefs were very strong;
They had a sense of right and wrong.
With compassion we see great concern;
It's not enough the facts to learn.
For compassion means that when we care,
We act instead of simply stare.
So let us pray with great compassion,
And let our lives by Christ be fashioned.
For God's compassion for our soul
Is what it took to make us whole.

GOD'S CALLING

What do you require of me,
Lord, I pray you'll help me see.
Let me know deep in my heart
My purpose and whatever part
That you are calling me to do.
Let me be one You work through.
Sometimes I think it's all so clear
The times I feel You really near.
It's then my life has balanced worth;
Your presence guides, I feel rebirth.
But other times I'm not so sure;
I'm overloaded, and life's a blur.
I know that feelings come and go,
Sometimes so happy; sometimes so low.
So, Lord, I pray you'll undergird
Your vessel, Lord, so what is heard
Is Your sweet Spirit in all things,
Your hope and peace and all it brings.
And use me daily for some good,
This much You've taught me that I should.
And if I'll put my faith in You,
You'll show me what You'd have me do.
And when You do, Lord, give me strength,
Your wisdom Lord to go the length.
To not go just by how I feel,
But to know Your calling is for real.
Everyday are gifts You've given.
Let's be mindful with our living.

GOD BROUGHT ME HERE

What has brought me to this place,
This time in life I seek God's face?
Why has my soul been aroused,
An emptiness that all my pals;
All my friends and loved ones too,
So much needed but they can't do
The work in me that I so need;
The grace of God my soul to feed.
At this time, I hope forever
God will guide me, leave me never.
So unworthy, my sin before me
I pray forgiveness, Lord, don't slay me.
Not just now I pray because
My heart's been opened to your love.
In this place I seek you out,
That You are here I have no doubt,
For I can feel Your precious Spirit;
Lord I long to be so near it
That the aroma of your love
Would fill my cup from up above;
That I would know the Son of God;
That Christ would be my anchor rod.
What has brought me here you ask,
A real sinner without the mask,
Here before God's Holy throne,
Pleading God make me His own?
So messed up and lost before,
Well, friend, my God stands at the door
And welcomes me just as I am.
I'm here because I know I can
Find renewal, strength, and love,
A brotherhood where people of
Different backgrounds come together
In Christ producing fragrant weather;
A sweet aroma God finds pleasing;
I, too, find my troubles easing.
In God's presence prayer is heard;
There's life worth living in His Word.
And here the praise of God is real;
I'm praising God His love I feel.
This place, my friend, is the place to be.
I'm serving God; enough of me.
And as I live, I pray I'll find
The Lord most often on my mind.
For when Christ lives within my heart,
Each place I go He'll not depart.
For my Lord has His hand on me;
From sin Christ's blood has set me free.

PRAY ABOUT IT

I am not a good example
So don't use me as a sample
Of what prayer life ought to be.
Instead it's Jesus you should see.
Although He was the Son of God,
To Him He never thought it odd
To spend much time to seek God's will.
He'd pray and pray and pray until
He found the answer that He needed.
What God showed Him He then completed.
Not an easy thing to do,
Distractions, always something new.
People pressing, crowding in,
The grimy world full of sin;
Full of need; He had compassion,
But prayer Christ found He couldn't ration.
He had to take some time each day
To let His Father show the way.
And God's way meant time on His knees,
Total focus, if you please.
It's then His faith found its renewal,
A means Christ found to be God's tool.
And though we're not the Son of Man,
Prayer is one way that we can
Keep in touch with our Creator.
Like our Lord, sooner or later
We'll find answers to our prayers.
We'll know more clearly our Lord cares.
So pray about it, your concerns.
By grace this privilege no one earns.
And while you're at it, give God praise;
He'll bless you, friend, in many ways.
You need not go this life alone;
The Lord is closer than a phone.
You reach Him on the wings of prayer,
And praise God He is always there.

THIS THANKSGIVING DAY

This Thanksgiving day I can say
Thank You, Lord, for the way
You've touched my heart with Your joy.
Your touch has healed; I'm Your employee.
I long to serve You as I should.
My prayer is simply that You would
Allow me to grow ever close
And lift You up so You're the most
Important factor in my life,
More than family, friends, or wife.
And as I seek to do Your will,
I pray Your Spirit will fulfill
In me the work You would have done,
And I praise Your name the work's begun.
I'm thankful for Your Holy Spirit.
This force of love from You, I cheer it,
For it has helped me through the greatest storm.
An ice-cold heart Your Spirit warmed.
So on this day I'm truly thankful,
Abundant grace, by the trunk full.
And not because I had the right,
But by grace Your Spirit gave me sight.
And now more than ever, I can see
Your love endures for souls like me.
Thank you, Lord, for all You've done,
And for Jesus Christ, Your precious Son.

WHEN WE FEEL GRITTY

On cloudy days
With rain and dew,
On stormy days
Just right for blues...

It's in the times
That look not pretty,
When life just grinds
And we feel gritty.

That we can choose
To rise above,
In fact to lose
Old Satan's shove.

For dismal outlooks
Is Satan's chore
Don't let his hooks
Beat down your door.

For you can pause
And take a spell
To bring your cause,
In fact to tell

Whatever problems
Got you down;
Whatever tends
To make you frown,

And go to prayer,
Someplace that's quiet
And go to prayer,
I urge you try it.

For we release
Old Satan's hold
He has no lease
When God is told.

For when we trust
In God above,
No little rust
Can stop His love.

And we will know
All fresh again,
Despite our foe,
With Christ we win.

WITH THANKFUL HEART LORD

All I have, Lord,
Is from You.
All I need, Lord,
You can do.

When I'm weak, Lord,
You give strength.
When I'm short, Lord,
You give length.

On my own, Lord,
I just fail.
On my own, Lord,
Leads towards jail.

Thanks for prayers, Lord,
You have heard.
I praise Your name, Lord,
For the Word.

Let me be, Lord,
All I can,
In every way, Lord,
Your own man.

With thankful heart, Lord,
Its my prayer
You'll light my path
So I'm aware.

That everywhere, Lord,
You're still there.
In trials sore, Lord,
You still care.

Because Your love, Lord,
Has lifted me,
I repent of sin, Lord,
Just for Thee.

And by your grace, Lord,
And my small faith,
We'll be a team, Lord,
In every place.

You'll live in me, Lord,
And I in you;
And where we go, Lord,
We'll go as two.

THE KEY

What is the key
To open up
The door to what you seek?
What is the key
To open up
God's peace week afterweek?

Is this, my friend,
Found in the world,
A key that money buys?
Is this, my friend,
Found in the world,
Just for the other guys?

The answer, friend,
My Bible says
Comes with persistent
    prayer.
The answer, friend,
My Bible says
Is with God's loving care.

God's loving care
We will receive:
The key each soul does need.
God's loving care
We will receive
If to our Lord we plead.

And when we're honest
With our God
We'll ask His will be done.
And when we're honest
With our God
His peace has just begun.

The key is faith
And daily prayer
To keep us right with God.
The key is faith
And daily prayer
To all who walk His sod.

To everyone
Who will believe
Christ died so they may live,
To everyone
Who will believe
By prayer our Lord will give.

He'll give the comfort
Of His grace,
His Holy Spirit, too.
He'll give the comfort
Of His grace,
The key to pull you through.

BROTHER'S PRAYER

Tonight another one led a prayer,
A servant of yours who does really care.
And while he prayed on bended knee,
All others had their mind on Thee.
And yet somehow my mind drifted,
Thoughts of my own were intertwisted.
I know Your love is a proven fact,
But tonight I wasn't making contact.
Is there space within me I want to hide,
Space to You I should confide?
Is there something separating me from You?
If so, I ask what should I do?
Does selfish pride get in the way,
And that's why I so often stray?
What ere the reason I was tuned out,
I pray, Lord, this you'll turn about.
For vocal prayers from a close brother
Reinforce a love for one another,
Directed to You but open to share.
Sincere prayers You answer in ways that are fair.
Holy Spirit, I need your help when others pray
And to direct my footsteps both night and day.

PRAYER TIME

No big deal in a sense,
But just the same you're feeling tense.
Little things have got you down.
It takes an effort not to frown.
Seasons of the soul on ice,
In no way can you say it's nice.
Reacting to disturbing news
Only brings about the blues.
And sometimes they are hard to shake;
There's only so much we can take.
And so it's natural we withdraw,
But in this story there's a flaw.
Because we needn't suffer long
If to the Lord, where we belong,
We place our burden in His lap,
And then refuse to take it back.
To faith the closest word is trust.
For our own good I think we must
Put our confidence in God,
And count Christ Jesus anchor rod;
To know that He will see us through,
And what He's promised He will do.
In storms, or even dreary days,
God has a multitude of ways
To bring renewal to our souls,
And minister to make us whole.
So won't you open up your heart,
To let God heal every part?
It all starts humbly when we pray.
Have you taken that time today?

1986 YEAR'S REVIEW

The Lord has helped me this past year.
His light inside has calmed my fear.
He has redirected inner anger
And pulled me safely out of danger.
Ones I loved walked out the door;
So the Holy Spirit helped me more.
The world dumped on me pollution,
But in Christ's love I found solution.
I cannot change the sinful past.
Only God can give me peace that lasts.
Forgiving ones that have done me wrong,
Was a way God gave me back my song.
Much time in prayer while on my knees,
Showed me Lord whom I should please.
So, Lord, I chose to be your man.
Your Spirit told me yes I can.
I can recover from life's setback.
Christ's love will heal is a fact.
The ones I love are a big concern.
I pray, dear Lord, of You they'll learn.
So, Lord, let me be Christ's example.
I want to be a worthy sample.
Help me rid all rot inside
And lead me gently by Your side.
And, Lord, I pray by this year's end,
My kids will know You as a friend.

VACATION

I feel today like standing still,
To halt the wheels of the mill.
I need some time to just relax,
To get away from all the facts.
Can hardly be to everyone
The guy who knows just where to run.
For sometimes I just hit the wall
And hope to God that I don't fall.
And for some time all that I've had
To warm my heart and make me glad,
Is faith in God to see me through,
And a woman's love which sticks like glue.
I don't deserve the joy I've felt
In how the Lord with me has dealt.
He's given me a new-found aim
To be His servant and to claim
The richest glories here on earth
That came when I received new birth.
But now it seems I'm at a place
Where I don't know just how to face
The task which stands in front of me:
Combine two families and serve Thee.
And perhaps I feel a little guilt;
There're gaping holes within the quilt.
A life which seeks to pattern Christ,
But is small in boldness like the mice.
Where to live, which job to find
Are playing heavily on my mind.
The talents God has blessed me with
Have through God's Spirit helped me live
A more rewarding sort of life;
But underneath there's still the strife.
So, Lord, I pray that with this day,
You'll refashion me in just the way
That will cause within me new desire
To take your love a little higher.
To trust you more and not to fret.
I'm trying Lord but not there yet;
But just the same I know you will,
For Lord you came to help the ill.

DRAW CLOSE TO GOD

I'd like to draw you close to God
If there's a way, however odd.
I'd like for you to feel His love
Descend on you from up above,
In the center of your being,
God His presence, healing, freeing,
Helping you in all you face
With you always every place.
I'd like to draw you close to God;
His perfect Spirit, never flawed;
Close to Jesus mind and soul;
The only One to make you whole.
Oh, friend, I pray that you can see
A part of Jesus lives in me.
No way perfect, still in process,
Life has taught me who the boss is.
I'd like to draw you close to God;
So close each moment you'd be awed
Not only by His works so great,
But by His love which shows you rate.
And because God holds you in esteem,
He seeks you'd join Him as a team
So you and I and millions more,
With Christ inside us and the door,
Would live to draw all close to God;
Our strength and help; our anchor rod.
For if we lived the way He taught
Our battles won would not be fought
By other means than prayer and faith;
God's Spirit leading our sure base.
For God knows full well what we need.
He brings to harvest planted seed.
I'd like to draw you close to God.
I pray His Spirit, not so odd,
Covers you from head to toe;
His love and grace so strong you know
Without a doubt you are forgiven;
Your debt Christ paid, now He is living
In your soul to complete His work;
God with you always, not some perk.
I pray we'll all draw close to God
For He lives and knows the road we've trod.
And He offers us a better way—
The road once dark now bright as day.

Growing In The Spirit

GOD-GRACED MOMENTS

God-graced moments
Oh, so real...
God-graced moments
We can feel.

Times when Spirit
Of the Son,
Close and near it
We are one.

A sweet accord,
God close and tender...
On us love poured;
Christ is the sender.

God-graced moments
Such as these,
In His presence
If you please,

We can glimpse,
See but a part,
But really sense
How great Thou art.

THE KINGDOM OF GOD

The Kingdom of God lives within each believer.
A spirit to serve God engulfs like a fever.
A desire to please the Lord, our creator—
No goal in life could be any greater.
Praise God with glories unbounded;
In Christ the Savior we are well-grounded.
The love of Jesus does in us abide;
It's a light to the world you cannot hide.
God's Spirit within won't stay bottled up.
God's love accepted will overflow your cup.
It's hard for a person lost in sin
To understand God's love for him.
How could God possibly care
For wretched men who are so unfair?
But He has a love for us we should cherish;
The Lord's will is that none should perish.
Removing Satan's firm grip on our lives,
God's Spirit conquers for husbands and wives.
God's Spirit is a heavenly blessing;
It will lift us though the world is pressing.
The Spirit will reveal the right from the wrong
If trusting in God our faith does belong.

HOLY SPIRIT

The Holy Spirit I have felt
When in God's presence I have knelt
And taken time for earnest prayer
Convinced that God would meet me there.
The Holy Spirit does not come
To casual seekers chewing gum
Who do not sense how great Thou Art
Nor feel remorse down in their heart.
For thoughts and actions they have done
That put to death God's chosen One.
For God, and Christ, and Holy Spirit
Indwell believers near it.
And where, oh God, can you be felt
If frozen hearts refuse to melt?
For those who fit into this mold
I urge you come into the fold
And make the choice to serve the Lord.
I guarantee you won't get bored.
And as the Lord lives in your heart,
The Holy Spirit will play a part
To do a cleansing work in you.
You'll know it for you'll feel brand new.

A HOLY GOD

As I walk upon earth's green sod,
I think upon a Holy God
Who cared enough to set me free,
Was not content to let me be.
A Holy God which art perfection...
To seek His presence my selection.
The Lord may call you, oh, so tender,
But He will never force surrender.
Our soul begins to come alive
When seeking God we daily strive.
We may pass through stormy weather,
But God alone will be forever.
Mortal men have numbered days.
Those in Christ will give Him praise.
For life may be short in years;
God's grace accepted calms our fears.
For if we follow Christ's example,
God's strength in us will be ample.
We can walk on higher ground
And all the while be heaven bound.
Christ was born that we might see
The love God has for you and me.
God is the maker of the earth.
His Spirit gives us second birth.
For Christ showed us how to live,
Abundant life with much to give.
Praise God first and to Him be true;
Treat others as you would have them treat you.
A Holy God remains the same;
If we're not close, our sin's to blame.
Christ is the way for closer kinship,
Through Him with God a two-way friendship.
A life with Christ is a new beginning.
With faith in Him we'll stop our sinning.
Time in prayer will bridge the gap,
And we'll be safely in God's lap.

CELEBRATE CHRIST

Haven't got it figured out
Problems that I see about.
Difficulties really near
Take their toll and rob my cheer.
Silly me I fall right in;
Brooding sometimes will begin.
Prayers unanswered have a cause;
Do they fit among God's laws?
I don't know, but I've been told
I will mellow when I'm old.
Nothing much will faze me then.
Gone will be the lure of sin.
But on the bright side let me say,
There is reason that today
I have hope and cause to cheer,
For my Christ is really near.
What He's done I can't forget;
His love and grace just do not quit.
So even as the heartache's come
I'm supported by the One:
The God of truth and light and mercy
Whose grace shows me that I am worthy
To cast my cares upon His lap,
And if I slip He'll take me back.
Yes, celebration lives within;
God's work in me He did begin
The moment I reached out in faith,
Thankful Christ did take my place
And bore the sin I couldn't carry;
Forgiven now, the past to bury.
Yes there's much that I don't know;
At times it seems that God is slow.
But just the same I know for sure
His love is constant and it's pure.
And though the gloom bug often knocks
As problems come like thorns and rocks,
The shield of Christ's own righteousness
Sees me through with His own bliss.
With celebration of God's love
I find that I can rise above
The world whose chatter never ends.
Praise God the Comforter He sends.
And praise to God He's here to stay;
We celebrate Christ is the way.

RETREAT

Sometimes we need to get away
And take some extra time to pray.
Most weekends seem to go so fast;
It seems they start, and then they're past.
But certain times we long remember;
The fire's gone, but still the embers
Remain inside to warm our hearts;
Recalling now, let's see the parts.
A retreat for Christian single folks
Renewed our strength and offered hopes.
The rainbow colors on each tag
Showed our worth, not where we lag.
A time to focus on God's love,
It is for us, not just above.
And then the hugs from caring people
Lifted us high as a steeple.
So my conclusion on this retreat
Is praise the Lord, why not repeat.
But as for me, I'd rather see
A home, a family, not just me.

SIMPLE FAITH

Don't know the scriptures really well,
But just the same it sure is swell
That God Almighty by His grace
Has given me the strength to face
The flow of problems of this life,
And pleasures, too, like my sweet wife.
With calm assurance in my mind
That God will be there in each bind,
It may seem silly to some folks
Who scoff and say it's just a hoax;
That all I've got is simple faith,
And real quick they'd make a case
That by the standards of this age,
My little life won't fill a page.
The mighty deeds and lofty goals,
Where are they brother?   No one knows.
Perhaps one day I'll pass on by
And folks may question "Who am I?"
But what's important in God's Book
Is: Did this fellow to Christ look?"
Did pleasing God account for much,
And did he pray to keep in touch?
And if by faith God's love received,
Did he pass on what he believed?
The point I'm trying hard to make
Is if your love for God's not fake,
Then He will use you right away
To build His Kingdom every day.
For Kingdom building is spreading love,
Through us by God from up above.
We needn't know all scripture verse
To break the Devil's little curse.
The only one we need at all
Is Christ within us walking tall.

GOD'S CHILD

You and I have missed the mark
We've done a few things in the dark.
Things for which we are not proud,
We wouldn't want them said aloud.
In fact we wish that no one knew
What's in the past we can't undo.
But past is past and here is now,
And God will work if we'll allow.
If we'll ask God to forgive
The shameful ways we sometimes live
And in our hearts invite Christ in,
That's when a cleansing will begin.
More than cleansing, brand new life,
A peace with God to end the strife.
Not perfected, nowhere near,
But whose child we are now is clear.
For when the Savior is our own,
His blood for our sin does atone.
No way earned, a gift of grace,
God's special love has earned a place
In our hearts, for He is good;
The joy comes out just like it should.
A child of God, a new beginning,
Precious grace to end the sinning.
Not all at once, but we will find
Christ brings renewal to our minds.
And when we seek His will be done
Life gets exciting and it's fun.
For we're not shackled to the past;
The old man died, we're free at last.
Every day a gift from God;
God's grace and mercy we applaud
By the way we share His gift;
Christ now within provides the lift.
Our friend, our Savior, and our Lord,
God's Holy Spirit keeps us moored;
Keeps us close if we'll just seek.
He's here for us week after week.
In fact we'll never be forsaken;
Christ is solid, never shaken.
He will make life worth the living,
Full of purpose and thanksgiving.

Chapter Five — Growing In The Spirit

IN ONE SPIRIT

In one Spirit
In one accord
Love poured out
Without a doubt
We could feel it.
God does heal it.
Thank you, Lord!

In one Spirit
Feel God's grace.
He is here
Gone is fear
Not by merit
But we share it
Who sees race

In one Spirit
Christ the center
Walls come down
To the ground
Almost hear it
Voice, no Spirit
God you enter.

In one Spirit
Praise your name.
Division goes;
Your love flows.
How we cheer it
Every bit
We're now the same

In one Spirit
The mountains move
We've changed for good
God said we would
Oh Father sear it
Our hearts spirit
Needs your groove

In one Spirit
In us deep
Have your way
Oh start today
Precious Spirit
Holy Spirit
Make us meek.

GOOD OL' FOLKS

There are a lot of folks we all know
Who are living right and walking tall.
They're never ones to brag and boast;
Their greatest pleasure is to be your host.
Good ol' men and women who may be plain,
But they'll take you in from the rain.
Living right does not concern money;
With all that we're taught that seems funny.
Character and principles go a long way
As to what people think and what they say.
Yes, I've known such simple folks;
What you see is real and not a hoax.
Some are young and some are old,
But this I've found which they all hold.
It's a love for God who's given them life.
God's love deep inside has surely eased the strife.
Good ol' folks aren't spared their share of woes,
But God's Spirit in them is so pleasant it shows.
So my advice if you're to be one of these,
Is to worship the Lord and for Him try to please.

PEACE COMES FROM WITHIN

Peace in this world is illusive
In fact it's hard to find.
It's more than being kind,
Or simply not abusive,
For peace comes from within

Just take a look around you,
Or simply read the news.
You're apt to get the blues
Before the day is through,
For peace comes from within.

I know surely as the sun will rise
That forces are in motion
Designed to cause commotion.
But letting them would not be wise,
For peace comes from within.

It's not to say that I've arrived
And nothing bothers me,
But brother I can see
In Whom peace is derived,
And peace comes from within.

The world's havoc steady stream
Can surely make you cringe
Or get drunk on a binge
If on Christ you do not lean,
For peace comes from within.

Within the circle of God's love
In quiet time of prayer
Is when we know He's there,
Beside us and above,
And peace comes from within.

And when we're walking close to God;
Close to His Spirit call,
And love Him most of all,
Then He's our anchor rod,
And peace comes from within.

For Christ in us defeats the woes
The world brings our way.
Praise God, He's here today.
Praise God, our cares He knows,
And peace comes from within.

Peace flowing calm within our heart
When we love God the most
And serve Him like a host.
It's then when He's a part,
That peace comes from within.

So, brother, let me offer you
The only peace I've known,
In whose Spirit I have grown.
Brother, let me pray with you
Till peace comes from within.

THERE ALL ALONG

It must have been there all along,
The gentle spirit and the song,
The love of God deep in my heart,
All along in me a part.
But some of it was kind of buried
Under sin and guilt I carried.
It had never surfaced long;
Can't say to God I did belong.
That's how I felt for many years.
Depression sometimes brought on tears.
But even then I sensed somehow
There's more than how I feel right now.
There's more to God than I can know;
I longed that He could come and show
Himself to me just plain as day,
But at the time I couldn't pray.
But life has ways to get to us;
We know when we have missed the bus.
There comes a time in God's own plan
When we will seek to be His man;
When we will get down on our knees
And beg forgiveness, if you please.
There comes a time we realize
Without God's grace we have no prize.
We have no reason to go on;
Only God can give us song,
Give us worth because we're His.
We saw the world. We saw it fizz.
But when by faith we saw the light,
Christ crucified to make us right;
The penalty for our sin paid;
That's when God shines in those He made.
The love and goodness God had planted,
In you and me, through Christ He granted
That we could live now by the Spirit;
God's call on our life, we could hear it.
Turning from the wrong to right
With our Savior light from night,
A different drummer now we hear.
God's presence now seems very near.
Just plain as day, God's now so real;
His love revealed, Christ is the Seal.
And if we'll give Him half a chance,
Christ will make our lives a dance.
We'll radiate His love inside
As doors of service open wide.
And we'll be blessed with life worth living,
God's grace so precious and forgiving.

POINT OF REFERENCE

I know you in certain ways,
The job you work on during days,
Perhaps just by the way you speak,
A southern drawl or maybe Greek.
A point of reference we all make,
Right or wrong, a big mistake
If by what little we discern
We judge, not giving you a turn
To share more fully who you are;
What light or beacon is your star.
To know what people are about
Takes some time, I have no doubt.
But over time a person's flavor
Will come out for us to savor.
We'll know where they are coming from,
If self and ego are the drum
That satisfies their hearts' desire,
Or if it's God who lights their fire.
What point of reference have you made;
What is your strength that will not fade?
For me the standard that holds up
Is Jesus Christ who fills my cup;
Who paid the price I couldn't pay,
My sins He bore and made a way
That I may live now by His Spirit,
Reminded grace, each day I'm near it,
All because of God's great love;
A reference point from up above.
My prayer is that God lead me straight,
Filled with His love, remove all hate.
And that the Spirit of the God's Son
Would dwell in me and be the One
That folks would see, not knowing much,
But glad at points our lives did touch,
Because the reference that was made
Showed love from God they wouldn't trade.
That's my goal; I'm not there yet.
But point of reference, I would bet
That Christ will finish what He started
In my life when He imparted
The seed of God's love in my heart.
He's never failed to do His part.

FROM HEAD TO HEART

I have heard, or I have read
The gospel message to my head
A lot of times; it wasn't new
I went to church, the thing to do
And I looked pious, in the choir
Among the guys my voice was higher
Praise to God was in the script
On Sunday morning I got dipped
A couple songs, some sermon sleep,
I was not about to get in deep
I'd pay my dues and get out quick.
Church was just a part-time fix
It allowed some social graces
I could put some names on faces
In my head, God's Word rang true,
But I had not been born anew.
I couldn't see my fallen state,
And made excuses; all men hate
And sins I knew were in my life
I blamed the fault lay with my wife.
So repentance to me didn't matter
Spiritually my walk was flatter
Than a pancake with no prayer.
How I needed grace and care!
The truth, my heart was cold as stone;
I'd tried and failed on my own.

Playing church was not the answer.
Only Christ could cure the cancer
Ripping this life wide apart.
I needed Jesus in my heart
So one day, broken, "Lord," I cried
"Please forgive; please do not hide
Your Spirit from me I repent
I welcome Jesus whom You sent
To pay the price I couldn't pay."
And suddenly it went away.
The burden carried all my days,
With tears of joy, in mysterious ways,
Christ had moved from head to heart,
And promised He would not depart.
It's where He always longed to be,
But getting there was up to me.
And so I ask, can you relate?
Am I alone who took the bait,
Who for so long thought it a game,
And was not concerned for me He came?
If this is you, oh friend, I plead
Go to Jesus, faith a seed
He will nurture and protect.
From head to heart, you will connect.
And when you do, on shouting ground,
You'll praise the Lord for whom you found.

VESSEL OF LOVE

Create in me a new clean heart,
Oh, God, I pray. Do not depart.
Cleanse my soul from head to toe;
Lord, your blood will make me whole.
Create in me the right desires;
I need you, Lord, to fan the fires;
To keep my purpose stay on Thee;
To from sin's bondage to be free.
You can do it, this I know.
It's by your Spirit I will grow.
It's your own goodness, not my own
That's lifted me and I have flown
In the Spirit with your grace,
Overcoming all I face.
Problems that defy solution,
A world of hurt with its pollution
Given over Lord to You.
You have solved and did renew.
My spirit broken You repaired.
I came to You and knew You cared.
Your Holy Spirit lifted me;
In Spirit, Lord, I now could see
That You were right beside me now,
Had been there all along somehow.
Even when I turned from You,
You sought me out and were not through.
For, Lord, this weak and sinful man,
Lord, you told me yes I can
Be a vessel of Your love.
You'd help me, Lord, from up above.
And, Lord, you've held Your end up well,
And I've improved and some can tell.
But, Lord, I've not arrived just yet;
The faults with me I sure would bet.
My desires, make them like Yours;
In faith let's walk on through those doors
Making life here somewhat better
With Christ our guide, a scarlet letter;
The Book of Life penned with His blood;
Such grace and mercy, like a flood
Does fill His sheep to overflowing.
God, You're good; please keep me growing.

CONFINES

We're all confined to some extent.
Our energy is quickly spent,
And we surely don't have all the answers
Like why some live or die of cancers.
And as new Christians you will find
God's Word comes slowly to our minds.
There're things about our Lord and Master
We can't handle any faster.
It sinks in more slowly than we like;
God's love and grace that give us sight;
Dimly, but at first a flicker
Forgiveness felt, a glow now quicker.
Jesus, slowly, in our spirit
Calling us, oh, can you hear it?
Yours and mine, our sins are nailed
At Calvary's cross, God never failed.
Still confined in many ways,
But peace now permeates our days.
For God is greater than our sin;
We know by grace He'll take us in.
When we repent and lean on Him,
The obstacles start getting thin.
For then we know that God is for us
And confines can't suppress the chorus
Of praise for God, the Great I Am,
Assured our lives fall into His plan.

EXPECTATIONS

We come expecting something great;
We've left behind all forms of hate.
In the spirit of God's love,
We radiate Him from above.
And when we do, wonders behold;
Another soul enters the fold.
A strong attraction in God's glory,
In these times we see the story
Brought to live, alive and fresh,
God intends for us to mesh;
To fellowship, give and receive,
Our faith is strengthened, I believe.
And when we hear the gospel preached
Expecting, hearing, we'll be reached.
And signs and wonders, they will follow;
We'll cling to God; all else is hollow.
Selfish motives, not for now.
Expecting God will move somehow,
Expecting God will hear our prayer;
And praise to God we feel His care
And have assurance God's in charge.
With Him no problem is too large.
And so it seems and so it is,
Expecting Christ we bring Him with
A welcome place deep in our heart,
And He responds to do His part.
Forgiving us, trespasses many,
In His presence there aren't any.
For God expects the price He paid
To set us free in Christ was laid
On the cross, for it is finished.
Space and time have not diminished;
For you and me, we can expect
God will do what's in the text.
He will live in you and me
As Christ becomes our seeing eye.
More in tune with other's needs,
Responding to them with our deeds;
Hurting in our brother's pain,
Using you and me He came.
Expecting God will act, oh, yes;
But He'll use His folks, us, to bless
And be the salt that gives life flavor.
Precious time with God to savor
And to follow up with care;
Expecting God, we found Him there.

BROTHERS IN CHRIST

Those who've known the risen Lord,
Christian people, love outpoured,
Reaching out to give a hand.
When I was hurting, understand
I didn't really know Him then.
Their Jesus, how can I begin
To tell you it's the God they knew
I wanted introduction to.
The peace, the confidence they had,
The love they showed, I sure was glad
That someone cared enough for me;
That Christ within them I could see.
How else, unworthy as I felt
Could God get close, until they knelt
With me in prayer to intercede;
To lift me up and meet my need?
And then to go the extra mile;
To be a friend and help me smile;
To be there when it counted most,
Humble servants who would not boast
About themselves, but would their Christ.
Through them into my heart they sliced
A portion of God's love, still growing;
Years later now, their Christ, I'm knowing.
Not completely, He's too big,
But when the fountain flows, I get a swig.
And when the Word of God takes root,
Forgive me, but I can't stay mute.
Christ has risen from the dead,
And Holy Spirit, like He said,
Has come to believers everywhere,
A blessed reminder of God's care.
And so, my friend, I come to you,
A humble sinner who's been brought to
My knees in shame; Christ gave me life.
He's also blessed me with my wife.
I found Him in great part by others,
For one in Christ, my friend, we're brothers.

SPIRIT-CENTERED MAN

At the center of the heart,
At the core there is a part—
The point from which we radiate;
It can lead towards love or hate.
Like a circle, if you will,
The center radiates until
The outward shape takes on the form:
What's inside becomes the norm.
And every person in like manner
Soon enough displays the banner
Which reveals what's inside,
For inner things can't always hide.
Is the center based on self,
Fortune seeking, and good health?
Does the center seek its gain,
Sometimes causing others pain?
Or has the center been transformed
By God's Spirit strangely warmed?
Has the Spirit of God's Son
Underneath the surface won?
It has if you've claimed Christ as Lord;
His saving grace will keep you moored.
Though troubles like the billowed sea
Will come in life, He'll set you free.
For centered in your spirit man
Is Jesus with the Master's Plan.
You're free to share your every trial
With God who'll walk with you each mile.
And when you do your focal point,
Christ-centered life God will anoint.
You'll still make errors by the score,
And sometimes willfully ignore
The higher calling on your life,
But you'll repent to end the strife.
For Jesus-centered means one thing:
God's love for others we're to bring.
And it's the circle of God's love
God wants us all partakers of.
We can if center-self steps down
And Christ within us shares His crown.
It's then His radiance folks will see
In believers, friend, like you and me.

REFRESHED

  Quiet and still is the current mood.
Times like this now are rare indeed.
A peaceful time in which I'll not brood;
More times like this my soul does need.

So much of my time is spent on the run,
A schedule to meet and places to go.
It's not all work and without any fun,
But it wearies soul and body, you know.

I think the Lord knows the balance we need.
When we're out of kilter, the time is still right
To slow down a bit and let the Lord lead.
Our spirit revives when the Lord's in our sight.

Of course, the Lord expects us to work.
To grow fat and lazy was never God's plan.
But work can get dreary; we need a perk.
God knows about this; He sent Jesus His man.

His calm assurance was that God really cares.
Contemplate that in the times of your leisure.
Body and spirit refreshed from life's snares,
Once more revived to be a God pleaser.

GOOD WORKS

Good works, good works, good works it seems
We'd like to do, they're in our dreams.
A mighty, noble work of art
That pleased you; it's in our heart.
To sacrifice and do without,
A labored love that comes about
Of mind and strength and iron will.
No peace or rest we'll find until,
Or so we think, the job is done.
Good works like this, they're sure no fun.
But then we reason it's required.
Christ paid the price, and we were hired
By God Almighty up above
To snap to with it. Show His love.
And good works seem the avenue
A child of God must surely do.
And while it's true there is some basis
As evidence in many cases
Of people changed by God's sweet grace—
That look, you see it in their face.
What follows, is it all thought out;
Or rather what God brings about?
Like fruit trees in their given time.
Produce a crop; they do not whine.
They bring forth the good work God intended;
And nourished right, the fruit is splendid.
Naturally and without a fuss
Good works come. God drives the bus.
It's Christ, the risen Lord, inside
Whose Spirit blooms, and now betide;
What God does through you, His branches;
Good works, fret not, for the ranch is
On good acres God does prune.
You're growing now and very soon
Good works that go beyond your being
You'll do. Praise God! It's Jesus freeing,
Setting forth His plan in motion.
It's more than us. It is an ocean.

THIS CHRISTIAN LIFE

This Christian life each day is new.
We're being formed by God into
A new creation He can use.
The grace of God has let us choose
To follow what we know is right
Or take the other path of night.
Being formed to Christian virtue
Is a process; it can hurt you
When you step outside His will.
You feel the pain, so real, until
You seek forgiveness and repent.
Your time in prayer is time well spent.
Christian life, it has rewards;
Away from self, you're moving towards
A life where service is the call.
In reaching out, you're standing tall.
And as you do, God fills your cup;
The peace and joy found isn't luck.
It comes from God who knows His own.
His Spirit lifts and they are grown
Into the image of His Son
Whose love extends to everyone.
The Christian life is not complete
Until all rests at Jesus' feet.

I NEVER NOTICED

I never noticed God at work
When I was down and I was hurt.
I only felt a pain so deep;
All dark inside and restless sleep,
Didn't help to lift the fog.
A beaten, broken, mangy dog
Best describes my outlook then.
The cause of all this was my sin.
I never noticed God's protection,
Or thought about the new direction
That circumstance as some would say
Made me look another way.
Too much of self to give God credit;
In God's permissive will He let it
Tear me up until one day
I cried, "Dear Lord, I'm here, OK?
I recognize I have no worth;
But Lord, please help, I need rebirth."
Funny, but right then I knew
God had heard and listened to
My plea and somehow by His grace
Caused my spirit, so off base
To waken to a brighter light;
A glimpse of God, just partial sight.
I never noticed, even then
That God was closer than my skin.
I only knew that He was real.
Praise God! Praise God! I had a feel
Of God's forgiving, grace and love.
I never noticed from above
The Holy Spirit called to me;
It's looking back that now I see
That even though I never noticed,
God was with me. He had floated
Life preserving help my way.
I love you, Lord. You heard my cry.

AWAKENING

It's kind of like you're in a stupor,
Vaguely thinking you are super.
But if you were, it made no sense;
Blinders, oh, my head is dense.
All the while I thought it cool
To live for self. I'm no one's fool.
Me And mine, that's all that counts.
Oh, Lord, forgive me, every ounce,
Thinking wrongly all because
I wasn't open to Your love
And what it was you had for me.
Blind and dense, oh, I'll agree
I didn't take the time it took
To ever read God's Holy Book.
And praising God was not my thing.
You ever heard the way I sing?
Call it stupid; say it's dumb,
Mistakenly I called it fun.
But what did selfish living bring?
Not much that counts for anything,
A broken home and years of waste.
No peace in anything I faced.
A God-sized hole within my life,
Jesus saw the sin and strife;
And praise God woke me from my sleep.
Awakening from hell so deep
One day I prayed, God set me free.
Please help me live my life for Thee.
Forgive me for my wretched past,
And help me know Your will at last.
And very sweetly, very still,
His grace, in prayer, not known until
That very moment touched my soul.
Christ died for me to make me whole.
Awakening, I saw the truth;
God cared enough to set me loose.
On Calvary's cross my sin debt paid;
A way to live for God was made.
The veil torn down which sets men free,
God let me know was torn for me.
And, friend, in case you haven't heard,
God loves your soul. It's in His Word.

CLEAN LIVING

Soap and water will do a good job
To clean the dirt off my skin,
But if I lie and others rob,
Who will save me from my sin?
Sometimes we'll try to fool others
To believing we're what we're not.
But Christ knows us more than our brothers,
All that's good and all that's rot.

When sin has us firmly in its grip,
Our conscience gives us little trouble.
"All men are evil," we may quip.
What's the use that I should struggle?
Or we may say, "I'm not that bad.
There're plenty of others worse than me."
But copping out makes our Lord sad.
He died, remember, to set us free.

Overt rebellion to God's Word,
Or pretending we're saved won't do.
But when we seek our prayers be heard,
The Lord will gladly help us through.
Obedience as God's own children
Means we should try to be a servant.
Selfishness gone brings on a grin.
We're heaven bound and not hell bent.

MY HELPER

My loving wife helps me a lot.
A Christian lady, she's been taught
Important principles of God;
Her help and stay and anchor rod
Is the Lord who sees her through.
Blessed wife, she loves me, too.
And likewise I can say the same;
Glad she shares my family name.
But I've another Helper, too,
I'd like to introduce to you.
A Helper you may also know,
The Holy Spirit. In His flow,
I've felt my Savior Jesus near.
He's blessed my soul and calmed my fear.
"The Comforter" to some He's called;
Source of grace to us installed
At the center of our being,
Pointing Christ toward; healing, freeing
Christian brothers from their sin;
Filled with Jesus deep within.
My Helper in this life of woe,
Jesus sent this much I know:
Third part of the Trinity.
This Helper's here for you and me.
When we pray, invite Him near.
In praise and worship one things clear:
We can feel God's loving touch.
How, precious Lord, we're loved so much!
My Helper's grieved when I do wrong.
He points it out and steals my song.
But He restores and fills my cup;
When I repent He lifts me up.
Help and wisdom, guidance pure,
Oh, friends in Christ, receive the cure.
The Helper sent at Pentecost,
Our compass so we'll not get lost.

THE PARSONAGE

Back years ago a preacher knocked
On my door and then we talked.
His wife had baked a lemon pie.
She asked us if we would stop by
The parsonage so she could cook
A meal for us; that's all it took.
Since then the parsonage invokes
Memories of the kindest folks
It's been my privilege to know.
Each family's helped my faith to grow.
Six pastors with their families,
In twenty years, all on their knees
At least one time have prayed for me.
I needed it, bet you'll agree.
In sermons now I can't remember
Living faith grew from an ember,
Planted by these Godly folks.
And in the parsonage my hopes
Were kindled one day I would see,
My home, like theirs, where Christ would be
The focus and the guiding light,
Which covers all both day and night.
So many great meals round the table,
Or watching TV; all had cable.
The parsonage I think became
A sort of refuge, in Christ's name.
Those who lived there asked me in;
We'd fellowship, rejoice, and then
God's Spirit filled our hearts with love.
It's all God's grace, I know, because
I wasn't worthy of such care.
I'm thankful Jesus met me there.

MADE WHOLE

Anticipating something great...
Good things come to those who wait,
And I've been waiting quite awhile.
To me it's been a long, long trial.
Trying ways to sort things out;
Faith that struggles with some doubt.
But I have been around enough
To know that when the going's tough
That God will somehow work for good
These circumstances like He should.
I don't know an awful lot,
But past is prologue and has taught
Me many times God will come through;
This time to teach me something new?
May be, but one thing is sure,
Faith in God for me is cure
For I know God is still in charge,
And His love for me very large;
Enough His Son hung on a tree
And died to pay the price for me.
Grace and mercy on my soul;
Lord You live; You make me whole.

GREEN-HAIRED PEOPLE

God loved you when you had green hair;
He loves you now that none is there.
For God sees things that others miss;
He's loved you always is my guess.

In fact the Bible clearly states
He loves us all. It's sin He hates.
By green-haired people I refer
To all the lost who never were

Living by the "Spirit's call",
Who thought of self and that was all.
Green-haired people are the ones,
The troubled folks God loved like sons;

Loved so much He sent His Own,
Christ Beloved to the throne
Of glory entered on a cross,
The Sacred Lamb, He paid the cost

So green-haired people and the rest,
For all of us He gave the best.
Sent a Savior for us all
Knowing man alone would fall.

Yes, God loved us when we were weird;
Yes, long before we ever neared
The place in life we sought Him out;
He cared for us and was about;

Right beside us in our trial
Protecting us so in awhile,
When we'd had enough of self,
He'd open up the greatest wealth,

The vast resources of His grace,
Forgiveness, cleansing, in His face.
When we repent, name Christ as Lord,
It's then His Spirit on us is poured.

Strength for the day, hope for tomorrow;
No more alone in joy or sorrow.
We have His Word to stand upon.
When all else fails, it keeps right on

Reminding us God knows us well,
And knowing all still chose to tell
Green-haired people everywhere
Let loose your sin; I really care.

I want to draw you close to Me.
I'll keep on knocking till you see
My grace will never let you down;
You cannot live until it's found.

And when my Spirit's in your heart,
I'll never leave; I'll never part.
For I chose you because I knew
You'd be a person I'd work through.

And one day when your work is done,
We'd be in heaven; two as one;
I in you and you in Me,
Just praising God for eternity.

EASY LIVING

Easy living. Is there really such a thing?
That's a good question, but what do I mean?
Easy for whom and what do they do?
It's a mystical goal many are after.
Will it make you happy? Give you laughter?
Advertisers promote it. Sales pitch won't quit.
More for yourself; boy, that's something!
Money, creature comforts; let's be king!
To achieve, many work hard; this is true.
Many others don't care whom they screw.
Easy is hard when it becomes your master.
Look out number one; pace grows faster.
Wrong priority; poorly written skit.
Put Christ first; get really lit!
Who says easy living is such a dream?
False prophet to me, it seems.
Bible teaches love God; this is true.
Treat others as you would have them treat you.
Follow Christ; find the life you are after.
In Him, victorious life, with the true Master.
Not easy living, but a life that is fit.
Serving God the Creator; giving more than we get.
The Lord wants you to be on His team.
Forget temporal values; serving others you'll beam.
God's love inside you, you can't stay blue.
Inner voice; Spirit within you is true.
God will save you; He's the Redeemer.
Accept His grace; don't be a schemer.
Forget easy living; it's the wrong trip.
Examine your heart; it's time to admit:
We're sinners, need a Savior, and love to bring.
Transformed heart, now real reason to sing.

OUR CHURCH

Johnston City has a church mighty fine.
It's on the corner of Broadway and Pine.
There folks have a deep love for the Lord,
Sometimes disagree but bound by this cord.
Like a family has ups and downs,
Most folks here have made the rounds.
Some get discouraged by the actions of others,
Especially those in Christ we think of as brothers.
Sometimes at odds and differing people,
Why do so many return to its steeple?
To me the reason is simple and clear:
It's the gospel message they've come to hear.
With an eye off others and fixed to the cross,
Folks get right with God and reach out to the lost.
Thank God for this church which is growing;
The Holy Spirit lets the love keep on flowing.
We ask forgiveness when we're out of God's will.
Sin in our lives causes spiritual ill.
As the body of Christ, Lord, help us do better;
Perhaps to the lonely send a friendly letter.
Let us reach out to people in need
And have no part of worldly greed.
First United has a purpose unfolding:
A beacon to others as God does the molding.
Helping hands is an excellent start.
It shows a love which comes from the heart.
Think on the message contained in this poem,
And as vessels for Christ together be rowing.

TRANSPARENT

Lots of truth people see
Soon after meeting you and me,
For we're transparent to a degree
The real me is what you see.
A gentle spirit, is it there?
Are we a person who does care?
Or are we mostly centered on
Ourselves? Thank you, and then we're gone?
So if it's true, like an open book,
We're figured out by those who look,
I pose a question God might ask.
Are you sufficient for the task?
So many hats we have to wear,
And burdens, more than we can bear;
At times it really is too much,
And we need much more than a crutch.
So transparent, full of need,
Of ourselves, is mostly greed
The trait most likely to shine forth?
Oh, friend, there is another course,
A plan the Father set in motion
With grace much deeper than an ocean.
All our sins put on the Son;
A ransom paid so everyone
Who'll confess Christ died for them,
He in no wise will then condemn.
Instead when to His door we knock,
His Kingdom to us He'll unlock.
Forgiven sinners have new life;
God's love lives in the man and wife.
Are we sufficient? No indeed!
But Christ, transparent, meets our need.
For with His Spirit in our heart,
Transparently He forms a part
Of who we are and where we're going...
Transparently, there in, our growing.

GOD'S LIGHT

Give praise to God who made us all.
His grace alone cushions our fall.
Without the Lord first on our mind,
We can get selfish and so unkind.
Life is full of daily troubles.
We need the Lord in all our struggles.
When our burdens become too much,
The Lord will help us with His touch.
Weak and sinful are natural men,
But reborn in Christ, sin cannot win.
Sure the temptation to sin will be there,
But we can resist by knowing God's there.
There to help us and be our best friend,
His love inside us will refashion our trend.
The ray of light that comes from God's Son
Will brighten our outlook towards everyone.
Once we accept we're all children of God,
And put our faith in Christ as we walk on His sod,
Then no matter how life's roadway may turn,
Christ's Spirit within us most will discern.

FORGIVENESS

Alive in God's Spirit is a wonderful feeling;
No aspect of life could be more appealing.
But how does one know if we're on the right path?
Is it real what we're feeling or only some flash?
Has God's Spirit spoken and had lasting effect,
Or has Satan convinced you you're just a defect?
I am a sinner who has been forgiven.
That saving grace from Christ has let me start living.
Forgiven by God I'm able to forgive others,
People in need I now think of as brothers.
The joy of the Lord must begin with me.
I must be willing to pay the fee.
Forgiving ourselves and those who've caused hurt,
Can come when we pray with our knees in the dirt.
And as we allow Christ to clean out the crud,
God's Spirit will enter our lives like a flood.
Suddenly we're awe-struck with the depth of God's love;
Our best friend on earth came down from above.
For the Spirit of God lives in the heart of the believer;
To do God's will becomes almost a fever.
If the Spirit we felt leads to brotherly love,
Then we'll know it was put there by the One up above,
And lives that are placed in God's fertile field
Can't help but grow fruits as to Him our lives yield.

AMAZED BY GRACE

There's not too much that God can't do;
You'd be amazed who He's worked through.
You'd be amazed the things God's done
In hearts of those who claim His Son.
There's one life that I know really well;
And that's my own, so let me tell
A portion of the grace I've felt,
When in God's presence low I knelt.
When all the world said, "Phil, you lost!"
God quickened to my soul the cost
That God had paid to set me free,
His only Son nailed to a tree.
The guilt of sin that long I carried
Repenting, God forgave and buried
Deep in His forgetful sea
And said, "By grace come follow Me."
Just when the door seemed shut and locked,
God gave assurance and we talked.
And then I found I had a friend,
Christ Jesus with me to the end.
And it's His Spirit, not my own
That God imparted from His throne.
God's grace and love to me seemed real;
His cleansing Spirit I could feel.
God's truth and light to me revealed
Christ was with me, not concealed.
My friend and helper in life's toil...
Always able, always loyal.
Without God's grace on my estate
Satan would turn gloom to hate.
But with His grace in this life's fight
I pray and hope you see His light.
Full of faults, but not the same,
From faith a flicker, now a flame.
God's love I cannot live without,
And that's what Christ is all about.

CALL JESUS

Very barren, cynical and dull
Becomes the soul till it's made whole.
For none of us who lives for long
Can help but see so much that's wrong.
And when the focus of our mind
Is stayed on this old earthly grind,
Then heaven help us, we are lost;
And when storms come, we're torn and tossed.
For very human are we all;
We need a friend whom we can call.
When all the world does let us down,
There's only One who'll stay around.
And unless we know this precious friend,
Our lives can come to no good end.
It might not happen overnight,
But then again you know it might.
So, friend, let me encourage you
To seek the Lord and be made new.
Refreshed by His eternal grace
He'll help you through the storms you face.
And you can know His steadfast love,
When more of Jesus you think of
Than any problem, place, or thing.
So why not give my Christ a ring?

WHAT'S DONE FOR GOD JUST GOES AROUND

It was just a couple weeks ago
When we were in this place,
I made a challenge you recall
For you to give our Lord your all.
The challenge came, I think you know,
And some could make a case
Because God's spirit lives in me
I pray that others too might see.

I asked specifically that night
That you would think about
What thing for God that you could do
Despite the trouble you've been through,
To spread a little of His light
Among the people on your route.
Because God's spirit lives in you,
I felt it was the thing to do.

We all are prone at certain times
To lose the broad perspective.
Some real problems close on us;
We wonder where we missed the bus.
Mistakes we've made require fines,
And, yes, it hurts down where we live.
But because God's spirit is alive,
We don't have to take a dive.

God's given us a choice to make;
He will not force our will.
We can acknowledge Christ as King,
Accept His love and praises sing.
Or we can go until we break,
And chase the world till we're ill.
Because God loves us all along,
We can love Him though we've been wrong.

We can thank God for life's sweet gift
And praise Him for His grace,
And with a small amount of faith
We can make progress in this place.
The heavy burden hard to lift
Is no longer such a case;
Because God's spirit lives in us
When we decide in God we'll trust.

By giving God the bigger part
Of the life He's given us,
We'll find the peace our soul is after;
We'll worship Christ as our dear Master.
Because His love has touched our heart,
We'll no longer want to cuss.
Because God's spirit is close by,
We can reach out if we'll just try.

And with some prayer and meditation
The challenge you have met.
And interesting I'm sure you've found,
What's done for God just goes around.
It brings you joy and gives you fun;
And also peace I'd safely bet,
Because God's spirit enters in
When we repent and lean on Him.

OUR LIFES WORK

"A life of work or our life's work,
Is there a difference?" asked the clerk.
"Looking over all I've done,"
He asked in jest, "had it been fun?"
"Well, yes and no," I had to say,
"But God was for me all the way."
Sometimes it's true I worked till frazzled;
All that effort; no one dazzled.
No one even seemed to care.
I'd question why God had me there.
Work, each week, to spread God's love,
Oh, Spirit, touch me from above.
For down here where we all must live,
We must partake before we give.
We need God's grace and mercy more
So we're refreshed to be used for
Something good within God's plan:
Our life's work to be God's man.
And though it takes all that we've got,
Our sins forgiven are blood bought.
And so our work should be no less
Than Christ puts in to help us bless.
And that's how daily work can lead
To life worthwhile filling need;
Not just for others, but ourselves.
Our life's work, the Spirit tells
In people living by their faith.
In Christ you'll see in every case
Greater love than was before.
Work, new meaning, now a door;
A way to spread the gospel truth,
Our real life's work that's of use,
In helping people grow in grace;
And that's a joy in every case.

GOD'S GOT A PART FOR YOU

God's got a part for you and me,
A place that we may serve.
He's got a plan
That every man
Can by His Spirit be
His vessel and His nerve.

When sensitive to God's great love,
God's love for every soul,
We come alive,
Begin to strive
To reach for things above,
To pray and be made whole.

It's not by chance that we were born.
God was there from the start.
He's with you now;
I know somehow
He'll be your stay from early morn,
With you He's now a part.

The Holy Spirit lets us see
By grace God does forgive.
Without that grace
We cannot face
A God who's paid the fee,
Who wants that we should live.

Abundantly with love inside,
With purpose, yes, we can.
We have the right,
Gone is the night
That grace so deep and wide,
It covers every man.

Who will confess, "Lord Christ, I'm yours?"
You died so I might live.
And you've called me,
Yes, I can be
The one that opens doors
To share and freely give.

CONDITION COVERED

My condition is not good;
Seems my head is made of wood.
For you would think from what I've learned
Completely from all sin I've turned.
Yes, I've blown it and been wrong.
In fact, my sin has stolen my song,
For lately I have strayed away
From Christ who saved me one fine day.
Condition, folks, is what you see,
But something greater covers me.
For while it's true I'm not perfected,
Christ in me is still reflected.
For grace of God and Christ's shed blood
Overflows me like a flood.
My position, saved by grace
Makes me not a hopeless case,
For on the day that I accepted
God in love had first selected
To sacrifice His only Son;
To pay the price for what I'd done.
Taws' on that day that God did start
A cleansing work deep in my heart.
And that position, saved by grace
Covers me; I have a place.
Yes, when conditions aren't so good,
And I've not acted like I should;
When sickness and the world's dirt
And my own actions tend to hurt,
God's Holy Spirit pulls me back
And fills in places where I lack.
And when repentance and my prayer
Is that God make me more aware
Of His great love and healing power,
And when I pray that love would flower,
And flow through me like He intends;
It's then a special gift He sends.
He shows me I may slip and fall,
But Jesus' shed blood covers all.

WAITING TILL READY

In God's timing there's a plan
For boys and girls, woman, man.
A time appointed when it's right
That we most clearly see the light.
The preparation to this stage
The Lord for each of us does gauge.
For God knows us right to the core;
He knows who's knocking at His door.
He knows the pain we've suffered through;
There're no surprises, nothing new.
For in God's wisdom He can see
The larger plan for you and me.
And there's a purpose for the wait;
God's timing, friend, is never late.
He comes to us when we are ready;
His grace sufficient remains steady.
And when the time for us is clear,
His Holy Spirit hovers near.
Our problems may still look the same,
But power comes in Jesus' name.
And when this truth we recognize
Our adversary, full of lies,
Becomes exposed so we can be
Equipped to fight, the Lord and I.
The time we lost cannot be gained,
But we no longer remain stained.
Forgiving grace once we've accepted
By God's love we stay connected.
And faith born out of trial and woe
The Lord did bless and help us grow.
The wait, though painful, till we called
The Lord allowed until we bowed,
And in our need called out to Him;
His plan for us goes back to then.
For born again is in God's plan.
Why wait, my friend, to be His man?
The time is now; you can be saved.
The road to heaven Jesus paved.
The waiting, friend, is our own choice.
Help us, Lord, to know your voice.
To know your Son is to know your Spirit.
Lord, help us daily to be near it.

HIS SPIRIT BECKONS EVERYDAY

I haven't been too spiritual;
My days of late have been too full.
I always have some place to go
Requiring that at least I show.
My time in prayer is rather short;
And visions, well, I'm not that sort.
And I don't broadcast very well
The love of Jesus I can tell.
So spiritually am I dried up,
No overflowing from my cup.
Have I received a portion slim,
Too much of me and less of Him?
Is Christ not master of my soul;
Has He just pieces, not the whole?
These questions, friend, I ask of you,
Concerning me and of you, too.
Because if you're honest with yourself,
Isn't Christ left on the shelf
Far more often than He should?
The price He paid was all He could.
His life was given for our own.
Forgiving us, God's love was shown.
God did it all and paid the price;
In Jesus, not born once but twice.
That's the reason we rejoice.
Our slate wiped clean, we have a choice:
To walk with Jesus everyday
Or let the world get in the way.
So spiritually the case is made.
Do we take personally the price God paid?
Is it settled in our mind and soul
That only Christ has made us whole?
If it is, friend, don't you worry;
You're not dried up and need not hurry.
Just let Jesus lead the way;
His Spirit beckons everyday.
Even days we're not on fire,
He seeks believers 'hearts' desire.

GOD NEEDS WOMEN

Women of the church rejoice;
Praise the Lord you've made your choice.
You've chosen life with Christ our Lord.
You've found with Him true love outpoured.
Every church in all the land,
In all God's Kingdom Christ has planned
That women have a central role:
That in their praise God they extol.
And in their acts of Christian love
Christ His glory from above,
Will pass through them, emit a flame;
Light of love in Jesus name,
A light that makes life worth the living,
Full of purpose, praise and giving.
For just as life comes from the womb;
Is nurtured there, each day fine-tuned,
Christian ladies with God's grace,
Those born again in Christ embrace
A kind of living, faith enriched,
That more than any sermon pitched
Causes others, family most
To see God's plan, the Lord of Host.
Little actions, thoughts and deeds,
Precious care this world needs.
Daughters, mothers, wives and friends,
Divorced or single, Christ attends.
And as forgiveness, grace and love
To them is shown from up above.
By God's Spirit ladies grow
And men and boys, they see; they know.
Kingdom builders God does bless;
Without the ladies, what a mess.
Without their witness where would we
The church of Jesus really be?
It'd be a Kingdom few would see,
Not that intended by God for me.
Christian ladies, rich or poor,
More than mothers God made for;
He's using you to do His work,
Essential, purposed, not some perk.
And you have reason for your praise:
God loves you now and all your days.

WE WIN

Using you, using me,
Catch the vision, can't you see?
God has purpose for us all,
Serving him we're walking tall.
For God chose us long before,
When we knew but did ignore;
When God's nudging on our life
Seemed a blur among the strife.
Even when we knew Him not,
God beside us saw our lot,
And with a love I can't explain,
Deep in sin is when He came.
When for no apparent reason,
God did meet us in our season.
In the time of grief and loss
God has chosen to bear our cross.
His forgiveness we received
When we prayed and first believed.
That God, His Son, and Holy Spirit,
Grace expressed and we are near it.
Grace poured out in such a flood
That you and I by Christ's shed blood
Can be a vessel God can use
To share His love with those we choose.
And if we need a new supply,
God will grant if we apply
If we'll let the Spirit lead,
Pray and God's Word also read;
If we'll choose our Lord to serve,
God in ways we don't deserve,
Will bless us daily in new ways.
His light shines upon our days.
And when the going gets really rough,
He'll give us strength and make us tough.
For its His grace and love we'll find
That brings us through the world's grind
And tells our spirit it is true:
Christ died for me. He died for you.
And He will hold us to the end;
If using us, we'll be His friend
And do the things that God desires;
We can so long as Christ inspires.
So long as we remain in Him,
No matter what, my friend, we win.

GOD'S PROMPTING

God gives prompting I believe,
Part of His vow He'll never leave;
Holy Spirit, like a whisper
Nudging you, God's calling mister.
Here's the answer to a prayer;
I heard and here's the proof I care.
Prompting sometimes seem so strange,
Like who but God could so arrange
To even enter in our head
To go and do something we dread—
Like mow the grass for Al next door;
He's sick, not ready for that chore.
And make a point to go see Charley,
Broke his leg riding that Harley.
And don't forget your Aunty Mack—
Respect her son and don't talk back.
Prompting, all of them for good;
Calling, saying these you should
Care about by taking action;
Shifting gears, faith getting traction.
Answered prayers you thus become
For others praying that someone
Would touch them at their point of need.
When you respond, you grow that seed
That builds their faith and makes them kind
And helps keep God fresh on their minds.
Your prayers and answers, now recall
How Christ who loves you heard them all.
And if not yet, He's still at work,
Prompting others to meet your hurt,
Or sometimes promoting you in ways
That when you listen within days
You'll find assurance God was there,
Directing answers to your prayer.
So listen, friend, God's prompting you
To be His vessels in all you do.

ORIENTED TO GOD

Out of this world we all come;
Its joys, its sorrows, and its fun.
We're born into the world we see,
With so much with emphasis on me.
To get ahead, we must look out
For number one or do without.
And so we find the world a grind;
In self no peace comes to our minds.
So, friend, how is your life today;
Have you found a better way?
I wonder how you're oriented.
Has your life been heaven-scented
By the fragrance of God's love;
Revealed through Christ, His grace above,
And all around, surrounding you;
Unearned grace which brings you to
A joy the world just can't provide;
Christ your helper and your guide.
Which road traveled are you on?
Has God's Spirit spoken or drawn
Oriented you to Him?
If not friend, why not begin
To admit you're lost and need God's help.
Tell the Lord the hurt you've felt.
And pray your sins that He forgive;
That with His grace He'd help you live,
Oriented towards His plan.
The good news is with Christ you can.

MEETING GOD TOGETHER

An island we're not meant to be,
All God's children, you and me.
It never was part of God's plan
For isolation among man.
And, furthermore, can't we agree
God's not content to let us be?
He's good at helping us find ways
To make Him part of all our days.
Time and time God's Spirit calls.
When we respond, His Spirit falls
And covers us with peace and love;
Not of the world, it's from above.
Sometimes in prayer when we're alone,
God's Spirit moves us to the bone.
We feel His love from head to toe;
His grace is there this much we know.
But, friend, sometimes we miss God's call
When we don't worship Him at all.
When we don't gather in His name,
We lose so much; it's not the same.
For men and women need to meet
To share and fellowship and greet,
To praise the Lord and hear His Word;
To share our faith and needs be heard.
We need to lift up one another
And show compassion for our brother,
And sing and praise and give God glory,
For in God's church this is the story.
This is the way that Christ did plan
His church, the rock, the hope of man.
For when in one accord we meet,
God's Spirit binds, and we're complete.
For what's bound on earth is bound in heaven,
And that fellowship is heaven's leaven.
It brings to rise before God's throne
A sweet aroma now our own.

GROWING IN AMAZING GRACE

I'm in process, not perfected.
Yet I'm glad, Lord, you selected
Little me, with all my doubt,
To show me what your love's about.
So unworthy of such grace,
In Spirit, Lord, I see Your face.
I see Your hand in all You've made.
You've answered me the times I've prayed.
Quiet times with You alone,
Your Spirit's touched me to the bone.
But still it's true, sometimes I'm weak.
Temptation comes, sometimes I peep,
Doing things I shouldn't do;
Sorry later when I'm through.
It's then, Lord, Your amazing grace
Helps me better see my place;
A man you love that You created,
Knowing all You've not abated.
Never holding back Your care,
You're steady, Lord, and You are fair.
Still in process, Lord, I know
With You You're wanting me to grow.
I know I've changed from what I was;
The difference, Lord, has been Your love.
And You no doubt can bring to pass
In my life fullness of a class
Which represents Your love in action.
Empower me to get more traction,
To be all you've called me to be,
With purpose and my faith in Thee.

DAY'S END

Can I be quite frank?
Right now my mind's a complete blank.
I've worked hard today.
I pray my kids are OK.
My, the sun's been hot!
I've given the job all I've got.
Now it's time to relax a bit;
Enough work, time to quit.
But even as I start to doze,
The love of God within me grows.
Each day is a gift from God.
Do you agree or find me odd?
On Mondays when I'm busy working,
God all around is always lurking.
He was there with dawn's first light,
And He's the One that gave me sight.
The food I ate He allowed to grow.
The beauty of nature is all His show.
My mind right now is not really clear,
But I feel the Lord is always near.
I know I don't always pray as I should;
I'd be closer to God if I would.
So, Lord, I thank You for days such as this.
You never said that all would be bliss,
But You'd be there within our reach.
Thank You, Lord! You're a peach.

JUST THINKING

It's kind of peaceful in this spot,
Gives me some time to think a lot.
I need some time to be alone,
Away from people and a phone.
I'm thankful for this springtime day,
And that the Lord's shown me the way
To live each day with blessed hope,
And to know with Christ that I can cope,
With whatever is next on my agenda,
And surprises which there seems no end of.
I love the Lord, and He loves me;
And folks I hope that you can see
God wants us all within His fold.
I've read the Word, and I've been told.
Yet sometimes I still have a doubt,
But God assures it will work out.
I thank the Lord for all His grace.
One day I pray I'll see His face.
But in the meantime, let me live
With Christ the Spirit I stick with.

God In Nature

GOD'S IN CHARGE

Calmness comes within our soul
When we know God has made us whole.
To know God's love we can't escape,
And that with Him it's not too late
To ever reach out for His touch;
It's settled God loves us too much
To leave us hanging high and dry;
I can't explain but let me try
To get across the joy I've felt,
When in God's presence I have knelt,
And asked that He would meet me there,
My sin confessed, I felt His care.
This life quickly passes by;
Oh, many things I question why.
Things for which no answer comes,
But in the breeze all nature hums.
God's in charge; He knows it all.
Who am I? I'm not that large;
But I am worthy in God's sight
For Him to comfort day and night.
Reflections cast from golden pond,
The fresh dew scent in summer's dawn,
In nature everywhere I look,
From stars at night to babbling brook.
In all creation Your work displayed,
And in Your image we are made.
It's much too much to comprehend
From the beginning to the end
To know that You won't ever change.
But in that knowledge it's not strange,
To say a certain peace is found.
My Lord, you'll always be around.

GOD WON'T LET GO

Lord, you've blessed me this fine day.
My heart rejoices for the way
That You have moved to intercede
To lift me up, my soul to feed
And let me know how much You care.
Today I'm blessed that You are there.
For me to sense You all about;
The earth, its beauty seems to shout
"I'm here in every leaf you see,
Each blade of grass, flower, or tree.
I made the rivers and the lakes,
The fish that swim, and, yes, the snakes.
Each living thing I did design."
The rainbow spectrum is a sign
That testifies how Great Thou Art,
Life giver, gracious from the start.
And, Lord, because You never change,
I know what's best You will arrange
For my own good despite myself.
You're here for me, not on a shelf,
Not a million miles away,
Your Spirit calls, "I'm here today."
To give me peace and let me know
No matter what, You won't let go.

QUIET TIME

Thank you, Lord, for quiet time.
It's then so often You do sign
Your handiwork which I can read;
The fragrant flower once a seed;
The bumble bee which makes his rounds.
And if you'll listen, nature's sounds;
Crickets chirping, rustling leaves;
The babbling brook, and swaying trees,
Quiet time to think and ponder;
God made all this, and stars up yonder.
Four seasons coming right in order;
Think about it, who's the mortar?
Who but God could bring it forth?
In quiet time we know, of course,
It's only God; we pause amazed.
And when we do, our spirit's raised.
For we know that He made us, too
These quiet times restore, renew.
They help us keep the right perspective;
God's in charge; He lets us live.
Quietly He fills our cup.
Once more restored we're looking up.

HOW FALLING LEAVES RELATE TO ME

The leaves remaining on the trees
Have lost the splendor that one sees
When they have just begun to turn,
And by this change what can we learn?
We know there's purpose in all things;
And dried up leaves, this, too, God brings.
For while it's true they make a mess,
The earth they touch they also bless.
They help to make the soil rich
And bring forth life at Spring's first twitch.
And the tree which sent them on their way
Renews itself with each new day.
For in the winter roots do grow,
And strength rebounds by winter's snow.
The dead leaf of itself is drab;
The parallel I hope you grab.
For like the tree, God made us, too.
He has a plan; things we should do.
And like fall colors, when born again,
All day our hearts just want to sing.
But we must die somewhat to self;
We're living now for someone else.
It's struck us we belong to God;
The love we feel isn't odd.
Now in this world so often cold,
We share God's love as He takes hold.
The sacrifice made in Christ's name
Can give life to the lost and lame.
Like fallen leaves enrich the earth,
A humble witness gives rebirth.
And even though the storms abound,
We'll grow in strength when Christ's around.
And like the trees resurrect in Spring,
Renewed by faith our spirits sing.

Chapter Six   **God In Nature**

IN EVERY SEASON

The cold of winter still drags on,
And we'll be thankful when it's gone.
The season leads to contemplation,
"Introspective searching," say some.
The frigid earth reminds our soul
That this old world can take its toll.
Like heavy ice can break tree branches,
Without God's Spirit there are chances
We will break, forsaking all
Numbed by life, but still God's call.
Still God's call seeks out the lost;
"Come to me; I paid the cost."
Cast your burden on the Son;
The Christ, the Lord, the only One
Who saw your need and then agreed
He'd do God's will. He'd hang and bleed.
A cruel death on a rugged cross
For you, for me, what have we lost?
For all of us God still calls out,
"Repent, old sinner, see the mount.
See the place you left me at;
The good news is I'm still at bat.
I'm still in charge, and you're forgiven.
I'll take you back, and let's start living.
If you'll not shut the door on me,
I'll help you live abundantly.
In every season, hot or cold
The more you let me, I will mold.
I, the Lord, won't force your hand;
But know this well, all you have planned
Will come to nothing in the end
If pride won't let you kneel and bend
To the lover of your soul;
The God who loves to make you whole;
The God who paid a price for you,
Nothing less than Christ would do."
And so you see, if you'll reflect
In winters our Lord will protect,
No matter what the Lord can see,
And He is there for you and me.
He knows our weakness and our faults,
And knowing all He still exalts
The glory of His Son in those
Who show Christ is the one they chose.
I'll be your own with all your needs.
It's then God's grace those needs exceed.

GOD'S LOVE IS ALL AROUND

The earth, the sea, the sky, the sun,
God's glory there for everyone.
In every living thing we see
A part of God's majesty.
The seasons which come right in order
Testify God is the mortar;
God who holds it all together;
God the source of all our weather.
God who gifted us with life,
Aware that we would soon find strife.
God of glory, God of hope
Made a way that we can cope.
God whose mercy far exceeds
Our failures, wants, and all our needs.
All combined in Christ His Son,
To earth He came for everyone.
God is grand beyond all measure;
His love through grace we all should treasure.
For in Christ Jesus we have found
The truth: God's love is all around.

SEASONS GOD MADE

It's freezing now, about to snow,
The last of fall's about to go.
The winter season soon to start,
And I am thankful in my heart
That all of this the Lord has made,
And though I freeze, I would not trade
The plan of seasons God designed
Over any wanderings of my mind.
For even if I had the power
To alter weather any hour,
I'd never in a hundred years
Make it right, despite my fears.
For God alone who makes the storm
Also chose that we be born.
And only God, who's always right
Can separate the day from night.
And He will reign forevermore
In seasons we're created for.
So we'd be best to smile and say,
"I'm glad God's given me this day.
And whatever weather He has chosen
I'll smile even if its frozen."

GOD IN SEASON

The dead of winter is a phase
That in our psyche kind of says,
"This is time that God just rests;
Springtime's when He brings His best."
When it's cold and snow just blows,
And the sun's not shone since heaven knows,
And you're growing weary in your fight
To just stay warm each day and night.
When rest is never quite enough
Because tomorrow out into this stuff
We must once more make our way
And struggle through another day.
Well, Lord, have mercy on our souls
For letting climate take its tolls;
For letting winter's blues set in,
Knowing that God loves us then,
And all the other days this year.
God never rests; He's still right here.
You, Oh Lord, are still in charge.
Your Holy Spirit's just as large.
And Jesus still sits on the Throne;
In winter's silence how it's known.
When we just pause, review the story,
By grace sin's covered; to God the glory.
By grace God loves us when we mumble;
So this, His season, let's be humble.
For God made every time of year;
Us, too, our thanks He'd like to hear.
For when we praise Him when it's cold,
Depression just will not take hold.
We'll see more clearly God's great plan
And cherish deeply His love for man.

THAT SUNSET WAS REALLY SOMETHING

The setting sun
So much aglow
Told this one
What I should know.

Once more in wonder
I did see
What any scoffer
Must agree,

That if the Lord
Were not at work
Something scored
Which made me perk.

The Something is
To my belief,
The God which lives
And gives relief.

A living God
That's far from dead,
That formed the sod
But never said,

"That I will ever
Leave your side,
But your soul I'll stir
So you can't hide."

And a way the Lord
Spoke to me tonight
In a sunset poured
Out light so bright,

And mingled with
The dusk's last rays,
Were clouds which give
Another phase

Of evidence all about
That God's in charge
There is no doubt.
No task with Him is too large.

God's all you've ever
Really needed;
So you should never
Feel cheated.

For the sunset that
He shared with me
Is also at
Your place to see.

And if you'll only,
Watch and listen,
You won't be lonely
For God will christen

Your heart with love
That's free by grace,
When God above
Reveals His face.

And through His Son
No better way,
The work's been done
So we might pray,

Directly to this our Lord,
The One who really cares;
Whose love He'll never hoard.
It's there for all to share.

Chapter Six **God In Nature**

THE WIND

I have never seen the wind
But I've seen what it does.
I've seen tree branches sway and bend
And sometimes break, you know, because

A mighty force you cannot see
Is present all around the place.
Its presence sometimes causes me
To head for safety just in case.

And in that place of safe retreat,
I'm thankful for the shelter there.
I'm thankful that the roof's complete,
And inside I've the best of care.

And like the wind, so is the Lord—
A God that none can see.
Just like you've heard a harpsichord,
You know what it must be.

The evidence is all around
This world our Lord did make.
And strangers are we till we've found
This all is for our sake.

And more than beauty of the earth
God offers us His grace.
And most of all by Jesus' birth
He shows us love so we can face

Whatever storms may blow our way.
Whatever we may have to face,
Because we know on such a day,
Our hope is on a solid base.

So if the world should tumble down,
And friends should all depart,
We know the One who wore a crown
Will be right with us when we start

To seek Him out in earnest prayer.
It's by God's gift of grace
That as we need His precious care,
We'll find the strength to cope and face

Whatever force may blow our way.
For Christ is with us all;
We need His victory each day,
And cleansing healing should we fall.

Chapter Six   **God In Nature**

GROWTH IN WINTER

In fall the leaves are on the ground,
A few of them on trees are found.
Mother Nature's turned her trick;
The branches now are bare and slick.
And now the rain is coming down,
And soon old winter with a gown
Of ice and sleet and snow and frost
Will chill the earth and all seems lost.
The growth, the beauty of the spring,
Is it in fact a onetime thing?
Or is growth sprouting when it's bleak; —
The beauty inside, so to speak.
In nature, friend, we know it's true
The roots grow deeper much like you.
Much like me when times are tough,
We break if we don't get enough
Of deep-down nurture from God's Word—
Like hidden rivers when it's heard.
It strengthens us and mends our soul;
The wreck you see is not the whole.
For inside, nurtured like the tree,
God's grace and mercy comfort me.
He strengthens me in times of trial,
Preparing me, so in awhile,
Like the leafless barren tree,
The growth is real, soon we'll see
The buds, the fruit, the work of grace,
The love of God upon each face.
Like trees, the beauty's always there.
God's wisdom constant, shows His care.
It's all in how you fix your gaze;
In Christ there's beauty all your days.

AUTUMN BLESSINGS

In Autumn leaves fall off the trees
When they are ready, if you please.
Just as sure as seasons change,
God causes leaves to rearrange.
They transform into fall-time splendor;
The colors show to us the Sender.
Only God could make a leaf,
God's handy work in each relief.
Each one different and yet the same,
For every leaf reveals God's name,
Has His signature inscribed.
In Autumn beauty God can't hide.
He's all around if we'll just look;
He made us, too, so says His Book.
And when the season's right for us
His gentle Spirit without fuss
Will whisper in our inner ear,
"I'm close. I love you. Do not fear."
We'll learn that God's own Word is true,
Perhaps to us, but it's not new.
In fact the process He did start
Was set in motion to win each heart.
For nature cries out, "God is love;"
We're all connected to the Lord above.
And when we'll let Him work His plan
In us his woman, in us his man,
He'll bring about a transformed self
Whose love for God is not on the shelf,
But seeking ways that we might serve,
For God shows love we don't deserve.
And as the seasons come and go,
With Christ as Savior we will grow.
Not all at once; we'll have our falls;
But we'll draw back as our God calls.
It's then He'll do what He does best.
His nature causes we'll be blessed.

SONLIGHT BREAKING THROUGH

This morning as I drove to work
I noticed beauty in the sky;
For light was breaking through the clouds,
In many places, bright and loud.
And I thought surely God does lurk
In His creation passing by.

The play of sunlight filtered through
Those multicolored puffs
Put some goose bumps down my spine
As I enjoyed the show so fine.
For what I witnessed helped renew
A love for God who's done enough.

A God who's given out of love
This world so full of bounty,
To us, His children, for its care,
And makes us everyday aware
That God's not only up above,
But He's in reach of you and me.

His presence, yes, is all around;
He hears our every prayer.
And when the storms of life appear,
And when we need Him, oh, so near,
It's then in seeking He is found.
It's Jesus, Son Light, blessed care.

Just like the light that broke through clouds
That filled the sky with beauty,
If we'll take Jesus to our heart;
If we'll let Him fill every part,
We'll be restored as heads are bowed,
And love will flow from heart, not duty.

And the life that God gave to us,
The life we thought all mine,
We'll want to say, "Now, God, take charge,
Let my love just grow, enlarge.
And help me not to rant and fuss,
But with you, Sonlight, clearly shine."

THE SQUIRREL

A squirrel is a joy to watch,
The way they run, then stop.
The way they scamper up a tree,
Then wave their furry tail to see.
A squirrel is a joy to watch;
We really like to see them hop.

When life seems sad and we are blue,
We'll often take more time to pray.
We need assurance God is near
To take away the dread and fear.
And sometimes on this rendezvous
A squirrel shows us it's OK.

For as the world spins and turns
And problems mount up everyday,
The squirrel plays and gathers nuts
And buries them in little ruts.
For life goes on the squirrel learns;
So work continues as they play.

The squirrel does what must be done
For winter's on the way.
By instinct they prepare a place
So they'll be safe, you know, in case
The cold of winter blocks the sun;
They're always ready for that day.

And likewise as a child of God,
Shouldn't we prepare today
To store God's goodness in our hearts,
To love and serve and do our part?
With Christ beside us where we trod,
God will supply and show a way.

And like the squirrel safe from harm
That's done his part each day,
If we'll just live as God intends,
By faith, with Christ, the Son He sends,
We'll enjoy life, safe in the arms
Of God, our Father, come what may.

SMOKY

This gray cat is my friend.
There isn't much he demands.
Food and water I must tend.
Soon in my lap he lands.

A shiny coat has this cat
And a motor that loves to purr.
Chasing mice he'll not get fat.
How he loves me to stroke his fur!

A substitute for wife and kids?
No way, but this I'll have to say:
When I come home, and I'm on the skids,
He lets me know that I'm OK.

This handsome cat I call Smoky.
He is a creature God has made.
In many ways he's, oh, so free.
To be like that, I need an aid.

With Christ I'm not a slave to sin.
God's Spirit in my breast does live.
Sometimes I get hit right on the chin,
But Christ inside has much to give.

A friend like Smoky in certain ways
Can comfort my soul in times of stress.
Smoky won't be with me in all my days,
But Christ will stick with me through every test.

So, Lord, I thank you for this gray ball.
I know you watch his every move.
And, Lord, I feel I've felt your call.
Let my life live within your groove.

Smoky only knows how to be a cat.
Let me, Lord, know to be a Christian.
I want my life to go like that.
Lord, let me hear your voice and listen.

SNOW

It's the first day of snow,
Kind'a pretty, you know.
Fun in the snow is an adventure,
All thanks to God it was sent here.
Hard to believe each flake is unique,
Made by the Lord we should all seek.
Nothing's so special about a snowfall
Until you consider who made it all.
Like the snow covers a barren landscape,
The Lord's all around; there is no escape.
Try as we will to avoid the Lord's beckon,
He'll get our attention somehow I reckon.
For just as the snow comes in its due season,
Our love's not complete till it's Jesus we're pleasing.
We expect the snow this time of year;
It's not a sight that we should fear.
So let the snow remind you all,
You're incomplete till you've felt God's call.

ICEBERGS

Icebergs floating on the sea
Miles wide, how can it be?
Some as big as many counties,
Vast and deep, a frozen bounty.
What you see, although immense,
Is just a portion of the dense
And larger hidden part below;
Where it ends, how can we know?
The iceberg, once part of the coast,
Has broken loose, and now the most
That it could ever hope to be
Is a frozen island whose telemetry
Can't help but drift to warmer waters,
There to melt as seals and otters
Rest and play on what is left,
Perhaps a few months at the best.
For icebergs cannot stand the heat;
The warmer currents do complete
The total breakdown of the whole,
The giant iceberg the ocean stole.
Icebergs are for us examples
Of unconnected broken samples,
Pieces broken from their source
That might and size can't change the course.
For no iceberg can live forever,
Once adrift is like you sever
Foot from leg or hand from arm;
It can't survive this full alarm.
And now let's draw a parallel.
Let's see what the icebergs tell
About the nature of creation,

We're in that picture, us, our station.
People God brought forth in love,
To Him connected from above.
The coast or mainland represents
Our source of being, God, and since
He has proven throughout time,
In every age He gives a sign
Of being steady, fair and just.
All nature speaks in God have trust.
Connected with God life endures;
With Him problems find their cures.
But when a break, like icebergs formed
Separate, no longer moored
In the household of the Lord;
Cast off, there's peril! All on board!
It doesn't matter what's the size;
Success without God: Titanic lies.
We may possess all world treasure,
But peace and joy they cannot measure.
For like icebergs they'll disappear,
Lost from God, in night and fear.
So what should we conclude from this?
I'd say that God we shouldn't miss.
That we should try to stay connected,
With faith and prayer, knowing God selected
Us to fellowship with Him
To find forgiveness for our sin.
So brother, sister, please don't be
A Godless iceberg lost at sea.

EARTHQUAKE

A killer quake has just occurred;
Folks very quickly got the word.
It's been a scene of grief and death;
On freeways many found their rest.
The final moments of their day
Came suddenly in such a way
They didn't have the time to pray,
Or ask that God would show a way
To help them in their sudden need.
God called before, but did they heed?
Let's pray they all have known the Lord,
And at this time are safely moored
Within the harbor of God's home,
That none of them had hearts of stone.
And so I ask, "How is your soul;
Has heaven yet become your goal?
Are you in love with your Creator,
And does that love each day grow greater?"
It will if you'll accept God's grace
And put your faith upon the base:
The solid rock of Christ the Lord;
Through Him true life, that vital cord,
That keeps your spirit right with God,
Through every shaking of the sod.

Chapter Six
God In Nature

THE STORM

I saw a mighty bolt of lightning
And heard an enormous thunder clap.
Then it rained so hard it was frightening.
Lost electric power as a final cap.

Not much of a story, heard a thousand times,
But each time I see it, I'm still amazed.
We're intelligent beings with superior minds,
Yet control a storm we've not fazed.

Do you suppose the storm has a purpose?
Perhaps God's reminding us who's in charge.
Sometimes our lives start to look like a circus
When we forget who's in charge and alone do barge.

It doesn't take a long life to learn
That there is only so much we can do on our own.
No wonder for God men do yearn.
Imagine calling God on the phone!

MOTHER EARTH

In all the universe there is no other place
As wondrous as our Mother Earth.
Beauty all around, the Lord shows His face—
Nothing more precious than a baby at birth.
The magic of water is a secret of life.
The key of joy comes in light.
To the self-centered, we end in strife.
Glowing with God's love on our flight...
Circumstances may seem crushing at times.
We don't know if we will ever make it.
Trust in God; know His signs.
Through adversity His love keeps us fit.

SPRINGTIME

As budding trees begin to bloom,
I welcome spring; it's none too soon.
I know we need the winter's ice,
But I find springtime twice as nice.
Much pleasure don't we all derive,
When all of nature comes alive?
I love to see our Lord's great work,
Especially girls in a short skirt.
To dig my toes into the sand
After winter is really grand.
For I prefer spring's gentle breeze,
Over ice and snow which makes me freeze.
So let me just express this thought:
I'm glad it's spring and winter not.

TIME OUT

I think I'll merely lay my head
Upon the ground and go to bed.
Today the sunshine and the air
Have prompted that I go out there—
Out to the park to pray and study,
No longer is it even muddy.
For this day really is the best.
I'll take some time now for a rest.

CHOICES

This sunny day makes me smile,
For it's been cold for quite a while;
And I know for sure it won't be long,
That the red-breast robin will chirp his song.
For springtime is just around the bend,
And God once more will flowers send,
And cause all nature to rejoice,
And so can we, we have that choice.
We have the choice to praise the Lord,
And we have the choice to cause discord.
We can choose to let God's love
Dwell in us from above,
And be a vessel full of light,
With love to reach out in the night,
And help another struggling soul;
To show their worth and make them whole.
The choice, you see, God gives to us,
But He lets us know whom we can trust.
For just as storms come from the north,
The springtime follows right on course.
For we can trust God's clockwork plan
Much more than any works of man;
And we can trust God's Word is true.
The choice is ours; what should we do?
There comes a time in each one's life
When choosing sides will cause us strife,
For the battle rages for our soul,
And until we're sold out, we're not whole.
Until our lives we give back to God,
In our hearts remains bleak winter's sod.
So why not choose to serve our Lord,
For an endless winter few can afford.

THE PARK

It's to the park I go each day
To eat my lunch, to read, and pray.
I'm glad I've found a place like this.
Without it, I would surely miss
The peace that comes when I'm alone,
Away from people and the phone,
And take those minutes that I need
To let God's Spirit take the lead.
For I must find a place to pray,
To let my Father show the way.
While at the park God speaks to me
In many details that I see:
The grass renewed each year in spring,
The birds that build their nests and sing
And pull the worms up from the ground
While squirrels gather nuts they've found.
The trees that offer blessed shade,
All remind me this God made.
And He made people that here play
In His image as a way
To show to me His precious love;
A love that I can partake of.
So I'll try always not to judge
Or hold for long a worthless grudge.
For I've found a better way to live,
To praise my Lord and from Him give
To others like He's given me:
That precious hope that lets one see
That God's great love and gift of grace
Is what we need in all we face.

Ministry To Others

DOING GOD'S WORK

We praise the Lord
For all He's done,
For comfort that
He sent to us.
For meeting us
When we were at
A place no fun,
And rain just poured.

We're thankful, God,
For what you've done:
Your Holy Spirit sent,
To comfort us;
To shine on us,
Lord, when we did repent.
You sent your precious Son,
A mighty anchor rod.

We honor You,
Most Holy God,
For comfort sent our way.
You're good to us.
You spoke to us
One blessed Holy day.
Your presence we applaud.
Lord, show us what to do.

We're thankful God
For your sweet grace
And mercies not deserved,
You gave to us;
You rescued us.
Lord, may we also serve,
With what we have to face?
Lord, can we join your squad?

And love my brothers
And comfort them,
And pray to bridge the gap...
Is this for us,
Yes, sinful us?
Your goodness can we tap?
The man from Bethlehem,
Will He help us save others?

And on all counts
The Bible's clear:
The answer, friend, is "Yes!"
What's done for us
Enables us
With Christ to have success,
To comfort and to cheer,
And evil to surmount.

So long as we
Keep Christ in mind.
And know what He has done...
He died for us.
He'll live in us,
For He's God's only Son.
What's lost He'll help you find.
By faith let's all agree.

BRINGING COMFORT

Basking in the sunny park
And viewing stars out after dark;
Finding time to just relax
Without a burden on our back;
Comfort like this we deserve
To charge our cells so we can serve.
For if we're worn down to the brink,
The chances are that we could sink
And be of little value then,
To both ourselves or other men.
Yes, we need to take a break,
But, friend, let's not make this mistake:
To think our goal is to recline
And to live for comfort is just fine.
For Christians God has plumbed a line;
A standard which will help define
How we should walk by God's grace;
It goes with us from place to place.
It says as people, God will cause
Our lives in Christ to show applause.
And the kind that touches Jesus' heart
Is when in Him we are a part
Of bringing comfort to the flock,
And sharing Christ, our solid rock.
In loving those God sends us to,
The faith goes on, it's born anew.
In others who were once in dark,
God's standard says you have the spark,
And don't you keep it to yourself
All bottled up and on the shelf.
The comfort God has blessed you with;
His love and grace, go share and live
It out in ways that point to Him,
For without God's light the world is dim.
So be a doer of the Word;
Share the best news you have heard.
Christ died to set the captives free;
Be comforted, that's you and me.

THE RIGHT TIME

This old joint is just no fun.
Oh, boy, would I sure like to run
A million miles away from here.
Do you reckon God would then be near?
At last my problems would be gone,
And I could face the morning's dawn
And say, "Lord, I'm just glad to be
Alive because, Lord, you created me.
And on that day when I'm set free,
I know I'll kneel and worship Thee,
And that will be my time of thanks;
No more will I play Satan's pranks.
Yes, in the future, Lord, you'll see,
I'll be the man you'd have me be,
And then I'll take more time to pray,
And let your Spirit guide my way.
Surely, Lord, you are aware
How tough it is to voice a prayer,
When my faith is sometimes so weak,
And non-believers call me a freak.
For to stand up, Lord, for Christ your Son,
Runs the risk that some will think me dumb.
So, Lord, I'm sure you'll understand
Why tomorrow's when I'll be your man.
But what if I should die today
Instead of later and miles away,
And I've not confessed all of my sin,
Nor asked Lord Christ to enter in?
Lord, will you still accept me then?
Though unredeemed, this joint's to blame.
Won't heaven still include my name?"
You know enough of God's own Word
To answer the questions you've just heard.
The time to get right with God is now.
His grace and your faith will work somehow
To supply you here and now with love,
The lasting kind, from God above.
So don't put off until tomorrow
The One who'll save your life much sorrow.

ON THE ROCKS

You're serving out a prison term;
Sometimes you're feeling like a worm.
It's not the place to brag and boast
On how you always got the most.
For if you reflect on this thought,
That you are here because you've not
Fully submitted to God's will,
It's wrecked your life and caused you ill.
And now the dangers, oh, so real...
The Devil's apt to make you feel,
That because you've made a big mistake,
God's not concerned with your heartache.
And if you walk around in shame
And hesitate when asked your name,
Then the Devil's pulled another trick,
For feeling worthless gives him a kick.
Old Satan would have you believe
God's forgiveness you will not receive.
A reject, no good, it's such a lie.
Such thoughts I pray you'll never buy.
God does not want to get even with you.
He wants to make you fresh and new.
A price for you God has paid.
The sacrifice for us was made
To show beyond the slightest doubt
His love for us is all about:
To be God's friend all you must do
Is accept the Christ who died for you;
That you are worthy in God's sight.
By prayer your pathway He will light.
For Jesus gave you this great power:
To be a living, growing flower.
A sweet aroma you will emit,
As more of Jesus you permit
To do a cleansing work in you.
His Spirit won't let you stay blue.
The truth is you have every right
To love the Lord with all your might.
When seeking God you will find
A peaceful sureness in your mind.
For those in Christ are not condemned;
By grace forgiven though you've sinned.
So reject Satan's strong approach
And let the Lord be your coach,
And you will find your life is blessed.
Even in prison you'll pass the test.
For God's own hand will cover you;
Each promise in His Word is true.

CALLING CARDS

"I know him," the people said.
"I'm sure no other one instead
Passed this way and left his mark.
I'd know it's he if it were dark."
Thoughtful actions, thoughtful deeds...
More concerned with others' needs...
A pattern noticed says in fact
This one's real and not an act.
A calling card I guess you'd say,
Showing you had been this way.
Not one printed real neat
With name and address all complete.
Not a card at all, I mean,
But something deeper, if not seen.
Call it, friend, just what you will,
But certain folks I think instill
To all who know those certain traits;
Some overlooked by loving mates;
The essence of a person's life
From where they are in all this strife.
Are they steady, fixed on Thee,
A shinning light that all can see?
Do their lives add up for good,
Helping out the best they could?
No, not judgments, just a thought:
Our calling cards, are they not
Showing people what we are,
A red, or blue, or silver star?
Or even golden, it could be
By trusting Christ with grace so free.
So, friend, consider marks you make.
Pray about the steps you take.
God will honor acts of faith.
These calling cards will leave a trace
Of blessings all along the way
Which show His people here today
Can live for God and show His glory.
The calling cards, they tell the story.

Scriptural reference: 2 Corinthians 3:1 - 6

PREACH THE GOSPEL EVERDAY.
IF NECESSARY, USE WORDS.

What have we been called to do?
To preach the gospel, very few.
But we've been called to spread God's love
With help from Him who reigns above.
Better than words, our actions speak
To others around us every week.
If God's own love we have received,
We'll spread that love, be not deceived.
For people know in really quick order
If you're for real, or on the border.
Are you consistent everyday
To help your neighbor and to pray?
Have you been seeking selfish gain
To others it's just real plain.
But if you really love the Lord,
Are close to Jesus, safely moored,
You'll preach the gospel everyday,
And not, my friend, by what you say.
Your actions will speak clearly enough;
You'll seldom stomp off in a huff.
But there'll be times, the Spirit leads
When the right words a person needs.
And then when words are necessary,
The light of Jesus' words will carry
From out of your mouth prayerfully
So others have a chance to see.

GO

Fourteen hundred times the Bible says "Go."
The Word never said we're just to sit.
The great commission's active verb is go.
We're not to be self-serving for what we can get.
Reaching out to others is the way to grow.
For by praying and helping one another,
We're behaving as Christians, don't you know.
So be active in striving to help a brother;
Listen close and respond to each plea.
Christ said as you help others, you're helping Me.

HANDS ACROSS AMERICA

Hands Across America was its name.
From all over America people came,
Joining hands as a gesture of caring,
For folks in America hungry and starving.
Many among us live on the brink.
Without some help they will surely sink.
People in America have a wonderful spirit.
They respond to needs whenever they hear it.
America among countries is quite mature.
We want to help and be part of the cure.
A nation of men and women under God,
Whose freedom-defending covered many in sod.
Hands held together for 4000 miles;
That's a record to go in the files.
People all different and in every color,
All of them Americans who came to help another.
This big country has people's needs pressing.
Holding hands helps and is a true blessing
Of a circle of help which forever needs spinning.
The Lord would approve what went on this day,
But it will take more. We all need to pray.

REACHING OUT

The wooden bowls the kids pass around
Each Sunday morning in them is found
Change, enough to make a difference.
It adds up fast: yes, ever since
This First United Church has started
Planning loose change be departed
From our pockets all for good,
Doing God's work as we should.
Advance giving surely has increased,
And it's not hurt us in the least.
The kids feel good that they can help.
Let's give some more, our hearts they melt.
And out there in the world someplace,
Real people who have a face
That chances in the bye and bye,
Will smile with hope because you and I
Did what Christ calls us to do.
We lent a hand, and in it grew.
Five stars aren't what it's about.
It's sharing Christ we have no doubt.

IMPERFECTION STILL GOD'S SELECTION

It seems no matter what I do,
How hard I work, when I am through
There are some things which need improvement.
It would take a real movement
Of God's Spirit in my life
To set me straight, remove all strife.
But I still get so disappointed.
Human, yes, but God's anointed.
Still the vessel God did choose
To do His work on earth and use
Talents that He's blessed me with
So His love through me He could give
To people not acquainted yet
With Christ, His grace, and I would bet,
Even though I'm far from perfect,
And often times so incorrect,
God's love still remains the same,
And He knows who I am by name.
And because His grace extends beyond
All my folly, it has dawned
In my spirit the God's truth;
God's loved us all from early youth.
And anything we do for Him,
God blesses, multiplies, and then
Brings to pass, don't ask me how;
His peace and joy for us right now.

IT'S NOT BRAINWASHING

Brainwashed was the word he used,
Mad because to him good news
Was just a ploy, an awful lie.
He couldn't see what you and I

Discovered mainly when God's Spirit
Got so close that we could hear it;
Forgiven by the grace of God,
Christ our Savior and anchor rod.

What is truth for you and me
Others blindly cannot see.
They think that I am just a fool,
And being Christian isn't cool.

Things of God so far removed,
Bitter life has not improved.
Needing Christ in the worst way,
But swearing never any day

Would they ever bow to Him.
They'll stick it out, however grim.
However dismal life may get,
They'll tell you back off, would you quit?

The ears are plugged, the mind is closed;
Unbelief, it's like they've dozed, Sleeping as it were through life,
A troubled sleep with too much strife.

Who is brainwashed, he or I?
"Maybe neither!", we both cry.
We both feel deep-down hurts,
Get charged at times in little spurts,

Inconsistent, full of folly
Subject to fall off the trolley.
So why should I care if he knows
Christ died for me; in Him one grows?

And He died for those who locked Him out,
Who never cared what He's about.
And Christ did it with the greatest love,
God calling us from above.

It's not brainwashing God is after,
Heaven knows it'd be much faster.
God wants us all to be His own.
That's why Christ Jesus did atone

And bridge the gap from us to God;
Such grace and mercy for the flawed;
A grace that even will reach out
To those who shun what He's about.

So let us reach out with compassion
To lost and hurting. Do not ration
The love God placed within your heart;
God's grace so large we've all a part.

NEW HOPE CHURCH

Visions come because a plan
Has shown itself that, yes, we can
Do the work God's called us to;
To be a people He works through.
That's not to say it's always easy.
Halfway efforts, kinda sleazy,
Won't please God. He wants our best.
When troubles come, we find our rest
And strength and hope to carry on:
In Christ, no other, He's our song.
He's the reason for New Hope.
Because Christ lives, it's in God's scope.
The care of people God loves so,
This place exists so they may grow.
So all of us and more forthcoming
Will grow in God, with praises humming,
And learn some skills and new behavior,
Jesus founded, in Him the flavor,
In leaning on the Word of God
We have New Hope, an anchor rod.
We have the Spirit God sends forth,
Jesus' flavor, right on course
Supplying all we truly need.
New Hope exists because a seed
Was planted sometime long ago,
And tiny faith the Lord helped grow.
And God's been faithful ever since;
It's Christ at work, make no pretense.
We have New Hope, and here today
We dedicate and hope and pray
That God will mold and shape this vision,
And New Hope Church without division
Will prosper as the Lord intends,
Meeting needs with those He sends,
And in God's timing, a full harvest,
New Hope beckons be our guest
To learn and worship, praise and grow
And feel God's love we'll have you know.

Dedication Service May 7, 1995

FAITHFUL LIVING

Faithful living sometimes means
Going forward when it seems
You've not made a bit of difference,
Wasted effort, so the inference.
Then the Devil tugs at you,
Why make an effort, nothing new.
Same old trick, full of lies,
But serving God is always wise.
If compassion you have shown
To a stranger hardly known,
Or God has helped you to forgive
The one who hurt you where you live.
And when you reach to help another
Because God said he is your brother,
Even when by each appearance
You should maybe give him clearance.
These are steps which show God's love
Have deeply touched you from above.
And they are steps, however small,
Which show to God you've heard His call.
Acts of kindness and of mercy,
Like God has shown to us, unworthy.
We now based upon God's grace
Can share His love with those we face.
And many times those most in need
Would turn to Christ if just a seed;
If just someone who knows the Savior
Would share His love by their behavior.
Through faithful living those we touch
We'll benefit by very much.
And after all, God brings the harvest;
We're just called to be the best
Person God made us to be.
And that's through Jesus, can't you see?

YOUR MINISTRY

God has plans for you and me,
In ministry, oh, can't you see?
Not all of us are called to preach
Or even go so far as teach,
But God has plans to use our lives,
Not just the husbands but also the wives.
And this is true for single folks,
Even you guys with your smokes.
Called by God to share His love,
To share His grace from above,
Knowing Christ has paid your bill,
The Father's plan He did fulfill.
And because your debt of sin He paid,
A brand new start at life is made.
Forgiven sinners, oh, praise God!
He chose you first, and we applaud.
We give our thanks and bless Him more
When we show others He's the door.
In ministry, that's what it's called;
To do it gifts have been installed
In the center of our being.
They give God glory when we're agreeing
To let His Sonshine flow through us;
To join the chorus, load the bus.
And from the cup which He supplies,
A river flowing never dies.
The Holy Spirit with you now
To comfort, guide, and help somehow...
Whichever way to meet the need,
To help believers plant God's seed...
In ministry, a life worth living.
God sees you this way; helping, giving.
For when the Lord has touched your soul,
It's then by sharing you're made whole.

For the staff of Restoring Hope Ministries
Pompano Beach, Florida

STAFF OF HOPE

Life in reaching out to others
God rewards, oh, sisters, brothers.
Be encouraged, all you staff;
It's OK for you to laugh.
Restoring Hope is what you do.
God supplies; it's nothing new.
He heard your prayer, oh, Brother Jack,
And you, too, Jerry, small setback,
God will overcome the trials.
Watch Him, Mona, bring on smiles.
Brother Leon, my good friend,
Thank you for the hope you send.
It's because you are sincere,
And Jesus you do hold so dear.
Ron, why question God at work?
He will fix whatever hurt
You have suffered in this life.
Christ brings the peace and ends the strife.
And, Larry, bless your very soul,
Helping others you're made whole.
Not so easy, but worthwhile,
Jeremy, now you have style.
Not the kind to push and shove,
You win the folks with constant love.
And, Will, you know Restoring Hope
Needs your wisdom just to cope.
In fact, dear staff and those to come,
God needs you all, yes, everyone.
He needs your prayers and faith in Him.
It's not by sight that you do win.
It's knowing in your hearts it's true
God's promises extend to you.
Don't be discouraged by your size,
But lean on Christ to make you wise.
Then He will open those doors
As into hearts pure love He pours.
Grace of God to pave the way,
Restoring Hope this very day.

WILLING SPIRIT

Are you willing to be used
For God's anointed plan?
Do you pray God's will be done
If it requires you be the one
That takes a with You, yes, I can
Attitude, I'll be your man?

When the cost means being bruised
For God's anointed plan,
We're criticized, and it's not fun;
And Satan's lies on us are spun
At times our spirit sorta ran
It's then, in prayer, Christ fires the fan.

Reassured by love we're soothed.
For God's anointed plan
Works through faith, and it is run
By willing spirits in the Son
Who venture knowing God won't ban
Access to the Great I Am.

For God sent Jesus to be used
For God's anointed plan
He prayed, "Thy will, not mine, be done."
The Spotless Lamb, He was the One;
The sacrifice, so we all can
Be willing spirits, in God's hand.

POSITIONED BY GOD

God's position is in charge.
No other kingdom is so large.
He owns it all we must agree.
It takes some time until we see
The only pose that's worth a hoot
Is one positioned, be astute,
That falls within the will of God.
We can know it isn't odd
Because God's Word has spelled it out.
Show His love to those about.
And then positioned by God's grace,
He comforts us in all we face.
And often times will do His work
Through those He's placed to heal the hurt,
To bring some light into the gloom;
To set the stage by making room
For His own Spirit to emerge.
"Be prayerful," comes the Spirit's urge.
It helps you be His emissary
With the good news that you carry.
Positioned then by God you'll find
A life in serving is the kind
That makes you happy, full, and blessed.
Positioned by God you're the best
At working out the great commission;
The gospel truth in love your mission.

GOSPEL SINGER

In others often times I see
The very opposite of me.
At least it seems to look that way.
Why, I recall the other day
At a concert in the park,
The singers radiated spark,
And sang in tune some gospel songs,
Too much applause among the throng
Of people gathered there in mass.
And I thought, "Boy, they've got some class."
Doing ministry like this,
In God's timing I would guess.
So good for them; they've got the call,
And they are giving it their all.
But if I use them, as a gauge
Of where I am upon life's stage,
Of how the Lord in me does work
In this old world with so much hurt;
Well, there God tells me don't compare.
What work I have for you is fair.
It doesn't matter in His book,
The numbers or just how I look,
But rather given where I'm at,
If for His Son I go to bat
And follow in the way He's leading;
Being there as folks are needing
Gifts of grace God sent my way,
There to share in love this day.
If we'll do that, we're in His will,
And we will grow in Christ until
Our purpose in Him is complete.
Then heaven's choir will sound so sweet.

CHOIR OF BELLS

Ever heard a choir of bells?
I tell you it's a treat,
For when you hear a choir of bells,
You'll say it's pretty neat.

Each one in the choir will ring
Two bells, but some have more.
The smallest shaken sounds a ding
Because that's what it's for.

Progressively up through the scale
Each bell it's certain tone,
When rung correctly will not fail.
They're made to be their own

Creation crafted with great care,
With each a work to do.
Each polished with a sound to share;
Oh, heavenly, I wish you knew

How a bell choir can sound
When it's all put together.
From bells that weigh more than a pound,
To some light as a feather,

Different, chiming, graceful notes.
It's music to the ears.
In harmony our spirit floats,
Exhilaration, moved to tears.

That's how bells well-orchestrated,
Ringing right on time
Can bless, my friend, as I have stated.
In fact it is divine.

Can spirit lessons here be drawn
From a bell choir's harmony?
What if timing was all wrong;
This picture could you see?

Big bells drowning out the small...
No order to the notes.
Noise, yes, but that is all—
Not fit for even goats.

Likewise, friend in Christ, I say,
"Your gifts, however swell,
Should be used in such a way
That folks can really tell

The glory goes to God above.
You are one of His flock.
And being sensitive in love,
In others you'll take stock

To complement and work together,
The Kingdom to proclaim.
God directed, may you never
Lose sight of your aim.

So share your gifts but don't forget
The choir God intends
Rings for Jesus so we'll get
Christ's brotherhood of friends."

ONE HUNDRED YEARS

In a hundred years who will know the difference
If in our short lives was Christian inference?
The world may still be spinning round,
But will Christian believers still be found?
Will people still know how to pray,
And praise the Lord we're made from clay?
And will God's own Word still be told
From true believers young and old?
In a hundred years if Christ's not come,
Will living waters still be sprung
From new believers just born again,
Led there by people wanting souls to win,
Into Christ's Kingdom begun long ago,
Person to person by folks in the know?
I think the lives that we're living now
Will influence later to whom folks bow.
And if God's Spirit now in us abides,
We'll produce for His Kingdom whatever betides.
And that work of grace now in lives taking place,
In a hundred years you could never replace.
For each Christ-touched life is a part of a chain
Linking generations of people with a heaven to gain.
And however short our seasons may be,
We'll still have an impact on all those set free.
So in a hundred years although our name be lost,
Souls touched by Christ's influence was well worth the cost.
For in a hundred years no life could begin
To repay our Lord who's overcome even sin.
Any difference we've made a hundred years from now
Will come from faith seeds our lives did plow.

Christian Celebration

PRAYERUL CHRISTMAS

Christmas time's once more arrived.
A year with Christ we have survived.
It's been a year of ups and downs;
Times we laugh and times we frown.
But in this season we remember
Our Lord was born so sweet and tender.
Born of Mary in a stable stall;
In Him God beckons us a call.
For Christ grew up and knew our pain,
And for our sins suffered without blame.
God in all His wondrous glory
Sent His Son to tell the story.
Jesus Christ was born the Word,
And prayers to Him are always heard.
Christ Jesus gives us precious hope;
What concerns us is within His scope.
If we'll just put our faith in Him,
In this life we can also win.
We win when love has found its way.
Our darkest nights turn into day.
For Christ alone can save our souls.
His Spirit lives to make us whole.
A busy season, but let's be careful
We're not too hurried to be prayerful.
Let us linger at that Bethlehem stable
And worship the Christ who made us able
To overcome the world and a life of sin
And give our lives meaning by His light within.
This Christmas let's express our joy
That Christ was born a little boy.

WHAT CHRISTMAS MEANS

It's Christmas day; I'm all alone.
I've tried, but there's no one to phone.
For every number that I dial
Just goes on ringing for awhile.
And so I pause and contemplate
On what's the reason for this date.
Why the tinsel and the tree
And little kids on Santa's knee?
The hustle now at last can cease;
I wonder will we now have peace.
And as I view the manger scene
And look out at the snow so clean,
The virgin child in the middle
Doesn't now seem, oh, so little.
For this day so long ago
He came that God we all could know.
He came as man, like you and me,
And showed God's love so all could see.
And now we try as best we can
To comprehend God's chosen plan.
And when by faith, perhaps a glance,
God speaks to us like in a trance,
And says, "Believe, for it is true;
For Jesus lived and died for you."
It's when God's spoken to our hearts
That Christmas isn't just a part
Of a year with many dates to fill,
But the day that all year long should thrill
The heart of every child of God;
For what He's done we all applaud.
For He has let His grace erase
The sins that we've smashed in His face.
The moment we embrace the King
Who loves us more than anything.
For when Christ Jesus has our heart,
It's then that we can do our part
To spread God's love to every soul,
And as we do, God makes us whole.

CHRISTMAS ROAD

We took a trip out to the coast;
We did it all, I mean almost.
We saw the sights from here to there;
The landscape showed us God does care.
And most important on our venture,
Smiling faces we did capture.
Locked within our minds we see
Memories spent with family.
My brothers, well, it's been five years.
And nephew, four, brought joyful tears.
And Mom and Dad, their love, it's grown.
Their love for me was early sown.
And now the road has brought us back.
I'm glad we ventured off the track.
I'm glad vacationing we found
God blessing people all around.
But there were problems, worries, too;
I prayed about to you know who.
My Dad who suffers from ill health
And problems caused by seeking wealth.
An uncle trying hard to cope,
He lost his wife and precious hope.
And sorrow, too, across the miles,
Like your family, mine has trials.
And so as Christmas season nears
Amid the joy, there're also tears.
But we are thankful God imparts
His grace through Christ to warm our hearts,
And shows to us His special love;
In flesh God joined us from above.
So as we journey Christmas road,
Let God's Spirit in us unfold.
For Christ whose birth we celebrate
Makes the season worth the wait.
For no matter what your station,
God is never on vacation.
He'll go with you until the end.
Christmas road means God's your friend.

LIGHT OF CHRISTMAS

This Christmas season I have found
There's not enough of George around;
For slim is how my wallet's been,
So why on my face the big grin?
Some needs are there that I can't fill,
And I've been too busy to sit still.
In fact in ways it's just too much,
So busy hardly time to touch.
Always in a rush it seems,
And bells are ringing in my dreams.
Busy, busy Christmas bustle,
Too tired at night to move a muscle.
But still the grin throughout the season,
I'm reminded of the reason.
It's not Saint Nick all dressed in red
Or reindeer flying with a sled.
The cookies, candies, and the snow...
The Christmas trees with lights that glow...
The children's laughter and the gifts...
The cards and parties, they all lift
Our spirits much, but it's all frill.
It's Christ's arrival the big thrill.
The old, old story once again
How God sent Jesus among men
To come alive within our hearts.
The love of God the Son imparts
To humankind which needs His touch.
Oh, praise the Lord His grace is such
That He reached out to save my soul;
Forgiving me He made me whole.
That's the reason for the grin;
Christ came to free us from our sin.
His birth speaks volumes to the fact
God loves us all by this great act.
The Christ the Virgin Mary bore
In Bethlehem that we adore
Was sent by God, alive in flesh:
The redeemer once our hearts confess
We're lost in darkness without His light.
Praise God this season it shines brightly.

JOHNSTON CITY CHRISTMAS

Just look around at all this beauty:
The tree with lights and angel cuties
The red poinsettias all in line,
The Christmas wreaths dressed up so fine.
We as people to this body,
Not all perfect, sometimes naughty,
Cannot help but feel God's Spirit
In this place. Oh, can you hear it?
Joy to the world, the King has come,
In Christ God's love for everyone.
Joy to the world, the Babe divine
Born Christmas Day! He's yours and mine.

CHRISTMAS EVE REFLECTION

It's Christmas Eve, the noon before.
I think about what went before.
The Christmas season so prolonged;
The merchants, boy, it seems they've wronged
The fundamental reason why
The Baby came for you and me.
In fact the Christ is seldom mentioned,
While cooking treats within our kitchen,
Or putting up the Christmas tree,
Or lights on rooftops all can see.
And even when the family meets,
Bare wood on pews, the vacant seats
Proclaim that most on Christmas Eve,
Their family nest refuse to leave.
No time it seems for such a matter.
Christmas bells and all the chatter
In the bustle of the season,
Have we, forgive us, lost the reason
For the celebration near?
Christmas Day will soon be here.
The joy of little tykes in glee
Who relish all the gifts they see
Should only add a portion slim
Of true joy found in knowing Him.
The birth of Jesus, God with us,
That's the reason for the fuss.
God loves us beyond all reason.
In our hearts, in every season
God made clear how much He cares.
Praise Him now; don't mind the stares.
Even if some call you crazy,
Do it now. Do not be lazy.
Worship Christ, the newborn King;
He gave to us His everything.
All for fallen, sinful men,
The price was paid. So, yes, we can
Walk in peace and joy and light.
Christ has come to end the night.

His name shall be called Wonderful,
Counselor, the Mighty God, The Everlasting
Father, The Prince of Peace. ISAIAH 9:6

AS CHRISTMAS NEARS

Christmas is but weeks away.
It won't just be another day.
It never is, you see, because
It celebrates the day that was
The birth of Jesus; God with us.
A quiet stillness and a hush
Overcome the shepherds there,
Before them answer to a prayer.
God, reveal Your glory bright.
The star of Bethlehem that night
Pointed to the stable low.
Wise men God allowed to know
A special gift God had delivered
Of a virgin, born the Word.
God's very imprint in the Son,
Born so sinners, everyone
Could be redeemed and have new life;
The lost, the lonely, man and wife.
Children, too, who hear His voice,
He calls and offers them a choice.
The Babe whose birth we celebrate
Would pay the price to end all hate;
Our sins forgiven all because
The grace of God had chosen love.
Born this day to make a way,
To save our souls. Oh, on the hay,
In that manger, born of Mary
Lay the Christ child, soon to carry
All your sin and all of mine
To the cross—God's plan divine.
So don't forget as Christmas nears
What be your lot, it's Christ who cheers
Our spirit all because He saw
Our need and freed us from the law.

CHRISTMAS ONCE MORE

Christmas is but days away,
And I am thankful I can say:
Despite the problems that I've had,
In my heart, rejoice, I'm glad—
Not because there's snow this year,
Or I have not a thing to fear,
And not because our tree is large,
And all are perfect in my charge.
No, the lights and glitter and Saint Nick
Aren't for me what does the trick;
Or that fills my heart with increased love.
That Spirit comes from up above.
It comes from God who's let me know
Christ the babe was born, did grow
Into the Savior for the lost;
That's all of us, and what a cost!
What a price the Lord did pay
So we'd be whole and find our way.
Grace abounding, love won out,
We know what God is all about.
This Christmas once more I'm reminded
That for my sin what Jesus did,
Was set me free so I'm no captive.
Love not passive but so active
I can't sit around and stew;
Forgiven, not just me, but you.
Rebellious children God still molds;
I must learn to free the holds
And let the Lord complete His task.
My prayer, God touch, is all I ask.

BLESSED NEW YEAR

The New Year started off today.
"What lies ahead?" You ask.
"Am I equal to the task?
Will God create a way?"

One thing's for sure you can admit:
Surprises are in store,
Perhaps more than before.
It seems they never quit.

Yes, there're problems out ahead
That's hand in hand with life;
But you can pass up lots of strife
If by God's Spirit you are led.

Some things you will have to do.
We all have obligations.
That's true in all the nations
For me and each of you.

But there's a Kingdom of God's love
Christ wants to lead us to.
He wants to make us new.
Our help comes from above.

The year ahead has now begun—
Can be for you the best
As measured by this test:
Did you accept God's Son?

In January when we freeze
And winter seems the hardest,
Jesus comforts and gives rest.
Our roots grow deeper like the trees.

And when the cold gives way to spring
And nature's beauty starts,
Christ quickens to our hearts
That serving Him is the greatest thing.

So as the summer heat begins,
Though sweaty we feel clean.
God's Spirit with us seen
In Christ we'll make new friends.

Forgiveness, grace, and love He holds
Each day for us to share.
As evidence God's care
And in the fall He molds.

So all year long let's say our prayers
That we might grow with God.
His glories let's applaud
For all year long God cares.

GOD'S NEW YEAR

A new year beckons you and me.
A clean slate—glory can it be
That how we live from this day forth
Can greatly change our present course?
Who says the past is locked on tight;
The old man can't improve his sight?
That what we were will always be?
Remember this: Christ set you free.
A new beginning in many ways,
A gift from God now marks your days.
For in you there is greater purpose.
Praise God, He looks beyond the surface.
For God sees things that we can't fathom;
Work divine for those who have Him.
And those that claim the Son of Man,
Look out, old world, for they can
Make a difference all for good.
When born again, God said they could
Move great mountains and heal the lame.
As Christ's disciples, we'll do the same.
The New Year which we enter in
Has purpose, Pilgrim, we can win
A peace we've never known before.
Look! Christ beckons at the door
Of our heart. Please let Me enter.
Give Me room, right at the center
Of your being, full of love.
This year you've help from above.
And even more, you're not alone;
A brighter spirit, a brighter tone
Will inhabit those in Him.
This year invite the Master in.

Chapter Eight   **Christian Celebration**

HATS OFF TO MOMS

"Hats off to moms!"
That's what I said.
Hats off to mom
Who made the bed.

A mother surely
Has much to do,
Beginning early
And all day through.

For mom wear hats—
More than you think,
Like ending spats
At roller rinks.

Now Mother's Day
At last is here;
So let's all say
These moms we cheer.

And here's a list;
Complete it's not,
To get the jest
Of what mom's got,

And what she's done
Because she cares.
No other one
Of self so shares.

Mom has a heart
That's full of love,
And she's so smart;
See what she does.

She'll feed the dog,
Work outside jobs,
The sink unclog,
Shucks corn off cobs.

Her schedule's full,
Enough to cry;
But watch her pull
And bake that pie.

A flair for fashion;
Wears panty hose...
With great compassion
She'll pick up clothes.

And Mom is thoughtful.
She'll mend your pants,
Cook till you're full
And water plants.

Laundry she'll fold,
And bandage cuts.
Sometimes she'll scold,
Pinch cheeks and butts.

Mom has her special,
Most favorite song.
It indwells her vessel
When things go wrong.

When writing checks,
Cleaning the floor,
And scrubbing necks,
And when we're poor,

She'll teach God's Word:
Show by example.
Each cry is heard.
Yes, she is ample,

To with God's help,
Supply our needs.
Her love is felt
Despite our deeds.

And the list is endless
Of what Mom does.
And we'd sure miss
Her just because,

If she should leave
Or pass on by,
She did believe
In you and me.

Her kids are worth
The world to her.
Yes, right from birth
We always were.

So, Mom, our hats
We lift to you.
For Mother that's
The thing to do.

But really what
Would make you smile
If like a nut
We'd walk your mile;

Put on your shoes
And do your job.
But, Mom, we choose
You not to rob.

For that's your gift,
A talent great.
So hats we lift
Because you rate.

MOTHER-DAUGHTER BANQUET

A Mother - Daughter banquet is
A perfect place to take this quiz.
So put your thinking caps on straight,
All losers must wash their own plate.
Who is it that makes a house a home,
With love remembered wherever we roam?
And who shows kindness when we fail
And stands by us to post the bail?
And, daughters, let me ask you this:
Who fixed your bruises with a kiss?
Who has the faith to see in you
More goodness than you ever knew?
And who alone in all this world
Will stay up late so your hair's curled?
And by her wisdom see your needs,
Then give assurance by words and deeds?
The answer, girls, is not your brother.
It's God's precious gift, your own sweet mother.

Victory In Jesus

WHAT JESUS MEANS TO ME

All babies are so very special.
In each small face all heaven echo's.
For you cannot look upon new birth
Without seeing heaven here on earth.
And though each child is ever sweet,
There is one I think especially neat,
For He was born the Son of God,
In our own image, kinda odd
To think that God would show Himself,
In a manger child lacking wealth.
All praise to God, He saw our need,
And sent us Jesus, here to lead,
A lost and troubled human band
To walk with God in every land.
And in whatever woes this life inflicts,
With faith in God there is a fix.
The birth of Jesus shows to me,
That God is real and Christ the key,
To a great salvation and purposed life.
With Christ we're born, not once, but twice.
For in Christ we see that God is love.
His Holy Spirit came with the dove.
And His love enfolds each new believer.
When born again, we catch the fever;
And a new desire to seek God's will,
Engulfs us for Christ has paid the bill.
Undeserved, unearned, by grace it's free—
Not to Christ, but for you and me.
So the birth of Christ, God's Holy Son,
Makes me happy, for He's the One,
Who transformed this once dreary soul,
Into a server, now made whole.

TOUCHED BY JESUS

Can you see a point in time
That God had given you a sign—
A special touch, a word, a lift
That caused your focus then to shift?
I recall it, oh, so clear,
A touch from Jesus, very dear.
Precious Lord, He touched my soul.
A broken man, He made me whole.
My life, it seemed, was at an end;
A cloud so dark that not a friend
Or any other force on earth
Could give me peace as that rebirth,
God gave to me when on my knee,
I prayed out loud to Thee.
Oh, God! Oh God! a wounded cry
Was my whole prayer; the Lord knew why.
The burden more than I could bear,
The next day overwhelmed, His care
Encompassed me, as from the air.
From every side I felt His love,
From top to bottom like a glove
That fits just perfect, custom made.
The Holy Spirit came to trade
My doubts, my fears, my shame, and hurt,
And anger, too, a world of dirt.
Just as I was, the Lord by grace
Filled my cup from His own vase.
And His vase never has an end;
A river pouring life He sends.
He poured it on me strong that day,
For my need Christ chose that way
To let me know that He was real,
And that in time my life He'd heal.
A shift occurred that day in me.
From head to heart I now could see
That Jesus did hold all the truth.
On His track I'd hitch my caboose.

This special day for me was March 9, 1986

HUNGRY SOULS

I see a lot of hungry souls
With longing faces quite intent
To be a little closer now;
To feel the love of God somehow.
The darkness black as southern coal
Needs that somehow light be sent.

For in these faces I can see
What every man longs for:
A purpose for the life within,
A freedom from besetting sin.
In you I see reflecting me;
In faith let's open up the door.

Let's all agree right from the start
Our basic human need:
A since of value and of worth
That's not connected to our purse.
We want to know what is our part.
We wish that God would lead.

The reason it's been hard for us
To know what is the truth
Is because we know ourselves.
Our actions sent off ringing bells
Which say we missed the bus,
For, boy, we are uncouth.

We feel that we're not good enough
To justify God's gracious love;
For we're unworthy, it is true.
Our guilt is on us like some glue.
So while we're scared we act real tough,
Afraid to call on God above.

But praise to God He knows us well,
For He created everyone.
And by His mercy loves us still,
Loves us despite our stubborn will.
So He sent Jesus here to tell
The battles over and He won.

For God's great love encircles all
Despite how much we try.
He only asks that we repent.
He only asks with Him time's spent.
He knew that man would fall,
That's why Christ had to die.

He took our place upon the tree
And suffered for our sin.
Christ died so we might live.
He died so we can give
Our love to others just as free
As to families, closest kin.

But there the story didn't end,
For Christ arose from the grave.
He won the victory! Praise the Lord!
For us there's victory, Praise the Lord!
He said, I am your friend.
My love and grace have made you brave.

GOD CAME DOWN

God came down.
He heard my cry.
He gave me real comfort.
Yes, heard my cry,
He came around,
And healed the part that hurt.

I know He did.
No other source,
No other power on earth,
Could change the course
To which I'd slid
And gave me new birth.

When the bottom had dropped out,
And life seemed at an end,
And nothing in this world could help,
I found a precious friend
I'd like to talk about,
Who sent me love I felt.

His name is Jesus,
God's Holy Son,
In spirit saved my life.
No other one
Could help this cuss
And put an end to strife.

His spirit said
"You're not alone,
And I your friend will be.
I hear your moan;
You must be fed
With love that comes from Me."

And praise to God
Who saw my need,
And heard my prayer, my plea.
When I agreed,
Knees on the sod,
My life I gave to Thee.

The burden lifted;
Was not my own,
God took the heavy end.
His grace was shown;
The focus shifted
As Christ became my friend.

And He alone
I soon found out,
Was bigger than the problem.
I have no doubt,
He'll hear your groan.
It doesn't matter when.

Just let your faith,
If just a seed,
To grow in silent prayer.
And, friend, your need,
Like in my case,
Christ will prevail there.

Chapter Nine   **Victory In Jesus**

THE DEVIL'S LIE

One big lie the Devil told
Has been told to people young and old
That is to say because we lie,
The Lord will surly pass us by.

The Devil says because of sin,
God's love for us we cannot win.
And because we've done such evil deeds,
The Lord can never meet our needs.

The Devil's good at casting doubt
That God cannot turn us about
For the Devil has a full-time job
Our peace with God he'd love to rob.

The Devil wants us in his camp,
Away from Jesus' shining lamp
For the Devil knows that Christ was right.
God loves us now with all His might

God loves us while we're still in sin
But wants the cleansing to begin.
So when we've finished out our years,
We'll join Him with our happy tears.

The Devil says you have no hope;
And if you believe it, you're the dope.
For millions of sinners just like you
Have found that God will see them through.

And the sin that's held us in firm grip
Will lose its hold and start to slip
Away from those who love the Lord.
With Christ we've found the saving cord

For when we've felt the love of God,
And His Holy Spirit has touched our bod',
And the smallest seed of faith takes root.
That our creator really gives a hoot

About me, the sinner, so unworthy.
Is it possible even I could serve Thee?
And the answer comes when once we pray,
And we include the Lord in every day.

We'll stop the lying and evil ways
Because it's true that Jesus saves.
That bitter darkness that was all we knew,
The Lord can pierce when He is through.

And the light that floods your soul and mind
Will make you happy and very kind.
So stop the Devil in his tracks.
Don't listen to his so-called facts.

Just believe by faith God's Word is true;
God loves you and can make you new—
Not on your own, but with His help.
So seek Him till His presence is felt.

When sought, the Lord will soon appear,
Close to your heart, He'll be that near.

HEAVEN'S LEAVEN

Daily life can take its toll.
God's Spirit sometimes doesn't flow
Inside us like we know it should.
Sometimes we wonder if we could
Erase the strife which we keep facing
And place our lives inside a casing
That keeps out all the barbs and thorns
And lets rejoicing be the norm.
Well, brother, you will never find
A perfect world unless you're blind,
And people will often let you down;
And in our tears we could drown.
If this old world with all its grief
Is where you're looking for relief,
Goods, money, or people, too,
Cannot help us when we are through.
For when at last our life is over,
We'll not live on fields of clover,
Or whatever word you use for Heaven,
Unless while living was "Heaven's leaven".
And "Heaven's leaven" in my view
Is the Jesus in you through and through.
For when the Lord is on your mind,
It's hard for you to act unkind.
He'll give your life that little lift
That comforts you though life may twist
And try to sap you of your joy,
And come at you with every ploy.
If you'll let Jesus be your casing,
He'll be with you in all you're facing.
And though the world won't go away,
Despite the problems you can say
I know I am a child of God,
And knowing this while on His sod
I'll try to walk in God's own glory
And tell the world the gospel story.
When "Heaven's leaven" is alive in you,
Despite the grind, you will pull through
For God knows the world we face each day.
He sent His Son to show the way.

Chapter Nine

Victory In Jesus

BEING GOD-CENTERED

In the center of God's will
I seek that place, and yet until
The Lord somehow opens my eyes
And I can know what's truth or lies,

The purposed-plan God has for me,
Until then, Godly help me be.
I see in part, some things are clear:
Be a witness, do not fear.

Use the talents I've been given
In help to others with their living;
Helping people find God's love.
This much was shown me from above.

But being centered, all of me
In God's will, how can this be?
In all my actions and my thoughts;
Jesus, help me. I need lots

Of help from You to just get by,
To pull the plank out of my eye.
To seek and find Your hidden treasure,
It's You, oh Lord, I need full measure.

Each day quickened to my soul
Your grace is what does make me whole.
It keeps me off the outer edge.
I'm trusting Jesus and His pledge

To never leave me or forsake;
Though looks deceive, it's no mistake.
The Holy Spirit dwells in me,
The only good part that you see

Is centered in the Son of Man.
It's faith in Him and in God's plan
That though I fail, He redeems.
To center in God's will it seems

Is a process that takes time.
This life, how much of it is mine?
How much of it belongs to God?
The center part, it's not so odd

Belongs no doubt to the Creator,
God's will, through Jesus, He be greater.
And praise to God, though not arrived
The joy in my life is derived

From walking in the light I'm shown:
Jesus loves me, be it known.
His shed blood has covered me,
Though not at center, I'm still free.

For sin no longer reigns supreme,
I know the Lord is on my team.
And with His help, one day I'll find
God's center will, and I will mind.

LET'S PRAISE THE LORD

Let's praise the Lord
Because of life
The beauty of the earth
Let's praise the Lord
For what He's done
For sending us His Son

Let's concentrate on Him alone
And not our poor estate
For God is worthy of our love
In nature how His love is shown
And when we praise and worship Him
No longer will we want to sin

All praise to God for His sweet grace
That we could never earn
Who's cared about us all along
Who wants to be the solid base
That we can always trust
In fact, in life we must

We must trust God to free ourselves
From all our wicked ways
And when we do, we'll find at last
Our purpose clear as ringing bells
That we were born to share God's love
And He will help us from above

So let's praise God this very hour
That Jesus showed the way
Let's praise the Lord with all our hearts
And feel His gentle loving power
And as we praise and give Him thanks
Let's let His Spirit fill those blanks

The doubts and fears we give to Him
Our sorrows and our pain
And, Lord, we give you what we have
And pray the cleansing will begin
And we will praise you all the more
For this is what you made us for

THE LORD IN MY LIFE

The world may press, but I'm set free
Because the Lord has been good to me.
The Holy Spirit has led the way
To seek God's will and then obey.
I could easily feel sorry for myself,
But God's love is inside, not on the shelf.
And so long as Jesus lives in my heart,
Each day is blessed before I start.
Even though life's storms continually brew,
I know the One who will see me through.
For the Lord who formed me from the dust
Is certainly One I can always trust.
He knows my needs before I pray
And wants to help me all the way.
A forgiven sinner is what I am.
By grace, God had a better plan.
His Son was sent not to condemn
But to free me from the sin within.
Bathed in Christ's blood I feel clean.
I know it's real and not a dream.
So if you long to share my blessings
And feel God's love in every testing,
Then confess your sins and ask forgiveness.
Make prayer the corner of your business.
And as you hold the Christ Jesus close,
Your heart will warm like fresh-popped toast.

PURPOSED LIFE

A life of purpose and of meaning
Only comes when we are leaning
On the One who loves our soul,
Our Lord who came to make us whole.
Purposed life will come about
When faith has overcome our doubt—
The faith that God whose grace exceeds
Our sins and failures and misdeeds,
A faith that tells us we're worthwhile,
That God intends to make us smile.
A purposed life will soon express
The love of God when we confess
That Jesus paid our debt in full.
That Satan's lies are so much bull;
That we can live and grow and serve;
That blessings that we don't deserve,
The Lord will nevertheless pour out
The more we know Him goes all doubt.
Purposed life that God approves
Is more to serve and less to use.
And when we find the avenue,
Our niche, the place God's called us to;
When talents that He's blessed us with,
We purposely and freely give;
Not so we will get the glory,
But that God, His love, in us the story
Will shine out and give Him credit;
It will if you will only let it.
Pray that God will let His grace
Clearly show upon your face.
It will when purpose He's designed
Floods your soul, your heart, your mind.

PROBLEM SOLVER

I can almost sort of say
Thanks for problems sent my way.
Not that they've been all that fun,
But they've made me lean on Number One.
For on my own without God's help
I'd never know the joy I've felt.
The sustaining strength God has provided
Came when all the world collided;
And problems like I'd never had,
Came at me both thick and wide.
Yet in the middle of this storm
Came Jesus in the kindest form.
His Holy Spirit was poured out on me,
Though weighed with problems I was free.
For in my spirit I was told
God loves me; I'm within His fold.
My life is not mine alone,
For God created every bone.
All I have is just a vessel
Which often times with God did wrestle.
"My will be done," I used to say,
Until one day I learned to pray.
Then Jesus became a vibrant force
Which put me on a steady course.
Confessing sins I did repent;
For such as I God's Son was sent
To show us all the love God holds
For each and every soul he molds.
And for those who fight Him every step
He loves them too, but what the heck!
He will not force His Spirit on them,
But He'll surely be there ready when
We reach the point we can't go on
And confess with Jesus we belong.
Though it's not easy, Christ was right;
He is the truth, the way, the light.
And by life's problems we can learn
To trust in God at every turn.

PEACE IN JESUS

Most of us without a clue
In this life just stumble through
Seeing not the larger plan,
Even wondering if we can
Get it fixed inside our head.
God's in charge; we shouldn't dread
Changes which occur so often,
Disappointments, what can soften?
What can comfort and bring peace,
Assurance and God's sweet release?
Grace of God, oh, what's it mean?
We know God's there but never seen.
And so a gap which must be filled,
For Satan's Devils to be stilled
Exist in you and me alike.
If God's not in it, guess who strikes?
Guess who gets the upper hand?
We know this isn't what God planned.
Grace of God, in parts we see,
Undeserved, God's good to me.
In God's debt, I know it's true,
What fills the gap and does renew;
Forgives my sins and sticks like glue,
Who is the beacon on the hill,
Who speaks and angry seas stand still.
If we'll just let our faith explore
God's Holy Word, we'll find the door.
And He's a person with a name
Who lives so we'll not be the same,
Who paid in full our debt of sin
And asks we place our trust in Him.
His name is Jesus, you'll recall.
He loves you even when you fall.
He came in peace not to condemn,
But to give us life and let us win
Battles that we face each day.
With Christ we'll surely find the way.
For in the Lord our God is known,
And in Him peace and love are shown.

LIVING BY FAITH

There was a time which I recall
When serving self was really all
I thought about or ever did;
Life's meaning still from me was hid.
I wasn't all that bad a guy;
Things happened and I wondered why.
Young and free without much care
It was seldom I took time for prayer,
For prayer I thought was not much use
To this cool dude, so I hung loose.
I had my health and pointed wit;
This world a stage and life a skit.
And so it went for many years;
I smoked and cussed and drank my beers.
And all my friends thought I was swell,
But on the inside I could tell
That something in my life was wrong;
Though blessed I really had no song.
And then one day I reached a place
Where only God could fill the space
And save me from my wretched state;
Then Jesus came to save my fate.
My inner man reached out in faith,
And I was saved by Jesus' grace.
And ever since that special day,
I've lived by faith, a better way.
The sin that ruled my life before
With Jesus was thrown out the door.
I'm still in process, not perfected
But I'm praising God I was selected
To be a vessel God could use.
But the choice was mine to choose.

CLOVER FIELDS

Have you been waiting for God to bless you?
Is all the rain getting you down?
Are the problems too big to chew?
Perhaps it's time to kneel to the ground.

Seldom does life go exactly as planned,
Of mice and men the saying goes.
Whom can we turn to when the door is slammed,
And we're crushed inside and no one knows?

Take heart, you pilgrim;
The battle's not over.
Just as a shepherd cares for his lamb,
Christ will lead you to fields of clover.

Things on the surface may seem pretty grim,
But knowing the Lord you're able to smile.
God's love for you does not ever dim.
He's right there beside you in every trial.

The world's good at tossing out curves,
But if like Jesus you strive to be,
Problems become avenues in which faith serves
To bring blessed light for all to see.

Do not wait for God to bless you.
Be a blessing, and you'll be blessed.
Clover fields are in the heart of men true,
To serving the Lord with their very best.

THE CROSS

Heavy, beaten, all worn down,
Mocked, despised, He wore a crown
Of thorns pushed down into His skull.
Upon a cross He hung until

The load He carried of our sin
Became too much for even Him
The cross was not a pretty sight—
On to it all the weight of night,

All the sorry lot of sin
Both now and what has always been
The death-like curse of fallen man,
Jesus bore; He said He can

Not my will but Thine be done
Oh, what a price, but let it come
A cruel cross, no mercy shown
The guards and mockers, should have known

That they had hung the Son of God.
In hands and feet they drove a rod,
And pierced His side and at His feet
Gambled for His robe as heat

From the pits of hell it seems
Put an end to all His dreams
If that were it, no Kingdom Come;
The Savior died so everyone,

Who had their faith His life had meant
God was with them, not content
To see us lost and without hope
Oh, look again. Oh, see the scope

Of how the Father gave His best
And to the end Christ passed the test
The perfect sacrifice of all
His perfect life paid for our fall

And in three days an empty tomb...
Life swallowed death and then made room
For you and me to overcome.
The battle's over, and Christ won

We needn't live in fear and doubt.
The sin we're born with found an out,
And that is Christ, in our lives Lord;
His Spirit moves us upwards towards

The Kingdom of His grace and love
It's for us now; not just above
Jesus, crucified for me!
It's in this act, oh, God I see

The length you went to set me free
Not content to let me be.
The price that I could never pay,
You did it all; you made a way.

And I will live now to your glory.
Unfold yourself, in us your story.
Love wins out because God cares
He always has. He heard our prayers.

DOING WHAT WE CAN'T

I can't change a single heart
To recognize they have a part
In the Kingdom of the Lord,
And that God's love on them is poured.
I can't do the Master's work:
Bringing comfort to the hurt,
And helping those who've lost their way
Take their need to God and pray.
In fact the gospel is too much
That I could ever even touch
On all the wisdom there to learn.
This grace of God I cannot earn
And turn from sin and start anew.
Oh, brother, I am asking you,
"Can it be within our reach,
The Holy Spirit there to teach
Our wayward soul the way to go
And know God's love has made us whole?"
I can't speak for you, my friend,
But I know I had reached the end,
And all my ways had brought me ruin.
The devil knew what he was doing.
But praise to God, I can't explain,
Christ saw need and knew my pain.
And out of mercy, out of grace,
He spoke forgiveness, in my place.
He paid a ransom I can't pay;
My sin debt paid, Christ made a way,
To do what we can't do alone.
Christ all sufficient did atone,
And breathe within us seeds of glory.
It's His plan, the old, old story:
All that we can't do for good,
Jesus in us like He should,
Grows and overcomes the bad.
Oh, Holy Spirit, take this lad.
Take this woman, take this man.
What we can't do we know You can.
And wonders will flow from your flock.
Can't beat my Savior, solid rock.

THE RIVER OF LIFE

River channels, they run deep.
The way we are, our course so steep,
From early years the pattern forms.
On our horizon, sun or storms,
Engraved it seems when we are young;
Our river channel then begun
Some kids learned from early days
That faithfulness to God's plan pays
And they received enough of Him
That living waters did begin
To have an impact down the road
Some kids do, this I've been told
But many more go on for years;
Their lives, their current, brings on tears
Their lives all theirs, full steam ahead,
Why fear the future, so instead
Of taking time to learn God's plan
Some went their own way because they can
I was in the latter group.
It hurts to tell how low I'd stoop.
Traveling down the road I saw,
Not concerned too much with law
Didn't really know the Lord,
Although His grace on me was poured
River channels, deep and wide...
The mess I'd made no one could hide—
Least of all, myself. I knew
My life in crisis through and through
Was sick of sin and self and grief
I cried to God to find relief.
Jesus, help me, I am lost.
The One who loves me I had crossed
God, I don't deserve your love,
And yet forgiveness from above
I felt; I knew; that Christ was Lord,
And He called me and moved me toward
A life of service, praise, and love;
His grace fit my need like a glove.
Unearned, its free; Christ paid the bill.
But lost and blind we are until
The revelation strikes our soul.
God loved me first and wants me whole.
And rivers, be they way off course,
Polluted, foul, with the wrong force,
Once they enter Jordan Valley,
By faith see Jesus, savior, ally
Miracles become the norm,
Lives transformed, the veil torn.
No more cut off from the Father,
Loving Him is not a bother.
The life, the river, God intended
In Jesus' care will soon be mended.
Is your river out of kilter?
Is gray how life looks through the filter
You've been looking through for years
Bringing you and others tears
If it is, my friend, let's pray
That God will open up a way
To help you see you're not alone—
That He is closer than your phone,
And He'll save you from sure destruction
In Christ the carpenter's construction
Never fails to turn the tide
Jesus saves the river wide.
And when your river flows with His,
Christ, your pilot, stays and lives.
Praise the Lord for this good news!
If Christ be for us, we can't lose.

HOLY SPIRIT COOKING

The Holy Spirit's working well.
There is a way that I can tell
When the Spirit of the Lord
Is in God's people, moving toward
The kind of love in action named
By Jesus, many times proclaimed.
Do unto others as you would
They do to you, if you could.
Place yourself within their shoes.
Oh, praise to God! I have good news.
There are people all around
Who live their lives on solid ground,
Helping out the best they can.
When they see need, it's in God's plan,
And help aplenty I've received.
A certain need has been relieved.
Friendly, caring, folks abound,
Many bringing food around
When my better half fell down
And broke her ankle on the ground,
Folks pitched in, cooking meals;
Good is how to us it feels.
Knowing people care enough
To stand by you when times are tough.

REVIVAL IN THE CAMP

A week of praise has just gone by,
So close to God it made us high.
The kindred fellowship was real;
The love of Christ is what we feel.
Five nights of seeing God in action,
Faith propelled just got some traction.
Gospel music mighty fine,
Prayer and praise most of the time,
With God's true Word so clearly spoke,
Into our spirits it did melt.
God loves us all and really cares;
With Him we'll beat the Devil's snares.
For God is good we have no doubt;
So many lost He's turned about.
Bringing light when none was there,
He saw our need and answered prayer.
A week that gave a lift much needed,
The love of Christ in hearts was seeded,
Preparing us for what's ahead:
The birth of Christ in a manger bed.
Revival spirit's in the Camp;
The Son of Man has lit His lamp.
He's calling us to change our ways.
When we repent, His Spirit stays.
When we walk closely with the Master,
Forgiveness comes a little faster.
The week just past has been a time
That we have seen that Christ is mine;
That He is yours, He loves us all.
He beckons, and we've heard the call.
Christ calls us all as little children.
From humble souls a Kingdom's building.
And this past week has helped us see
God's plan has room for you and me.
We praise the Lord for His sweet Spirit.
Thank you, Lord, we've been so near it.

THERE'S A REASON I STILL RHYME

Doing things to fill up time...
Trying hard to stay on line...
Being square, is that a crime?
I'm trying not to sink in slime.

My life has had its up and downs;
I've fallen times and smashed my crown.
Sometimes it's hard not to frown,
But there's a reason I still rhyme.

For in this life of broken dreams,
It 's really not all that it seems.
Despite our wayward awkward schemes,
There's one whose love is always kind.

Jesus is the One I've found
Who knows the reason I've been bound,
And came to save me - every pound.
He's been really heavy on my mind.

Was for my sins He hung and died,
When I was hurting , He too cried.
He knew my need and took my side.
In forgiving me, God's love I find.

All around me I have seen
Worldly people acting mean
While thinking that their ways are keen.
Lord, help them for their spirit's blind.

And help me, too, that I might see
The better life Christ has for me.
If I will serve and choose to be
God's light reflector in every bind.

HAPPINESS

People spend a lot of dough
To be happy, don't you know?
And who can say that they are wrong?
Each of us deserves a song.
Each of us. Calls it a right,
Needs a happy, shining light,
Needs to feel so worthwhile...
We can't help but often smile.
Some try drugs, some try booze,
And some try sex with whom they choose.
And self-help books, a zillion score,
Tomorrow, no doubt, thousands more...
Happiness, for some it seems,
Only exists in their dreams;
And in their hopes to have it all,
They set themselves up for a fall.
Power, wealth, and health can't be
The all it takes to make you free,
To satisfy your deepest need,
Or even keep up with your greed.
Happiness I think evolves
When burdens given our Lord solves.
It comes about with some assurance
God's love is here in present tense.
That though we fail and miss the mark,
He'll not leave us in the dark.
True happiness comes in the knowing
God is watching and is growing
Faith in us to do His work.
It satisfies more than some perk
That comes from having larger toys
Or getting loud out with the boys.
Happiness comes from within
And our relationship to Him.
It's Jesus Christ I'm speaking of.
Be blessed and happy in His love.

EDUCATION REFLECTION

I went to college some years back,
So long ago I've lost contact,
With all the friends there I once knew.
But I remember what I went through:
Four long years of classroom study
And books became my closest buddy.
They had a way to stretch my mind,
But peace with them I could not find.
In college I learned many things,
But not the joy that Jesus brings.
My education lacked His voice.
I'm part to blame; I made a choice.
My ignorance had me believe
We're blessed by how much we receive.
And he who's mastered college arts
Will surely be blessed by getting smarts.
Well, college days are long since past.
I'm forty now; time's flown that fast.
It's time to ask this simple query:
Did my sheepskin match up to the theory,
That open doors would soon appear,
And when I walked in, they all would cheer?
Well seeing things from my perspective,
The theory's wrong and so defective.
For we are best prepared for life
When we've awakened to the living Christ.
When serving God's our worthy goal,
Our serving Him helps make us whole.
And until one learns these Bible truths,
Our education cannot produce
A happy life with true success—
Success measured by how we serve,
Not just seeking what we "deserve."
My education just began
When I asked Christ to take my hand.

JESUS STREET

Just looking down the happy street,
The grass and trees and folks you meet,
The houses fixed up kind of cute
Would seem to say to those astute
That people living on this block,
Who work and give their dogs a walk,
Whose kids attend the local school,
And some enjoy their backyard pool;
That these blessed souls from what we see
Are just as happy as could be.
But if we take a second look,
We'll find there're things that we mistook.
For every soul that we pass by,
Yes, even folks who wave us "hi",
That all of these and those unseen
Have hurts and problems, sometimes mean.
For they like you, and me the same
Have walked sometimes through freezing rain.
And every life has its own storm;
To say we're living says we're worn.
But worn and torn are not the same.
The blessed here know Jesus' name.
Though all of us be tossed about,
The hurts don't heal if we're without
The Savior living in our heart,
His love and grace to us impart,
The flow of goodness, God's own breath,
To those who pray and sins confess.
The troubles come to all who live,
But Jesus' open arms forgive.
So if the street you happen on
Looks good but, all the joy is gone,
Or if there're ruts and home's a shack
Where Satan's been on the attack;
Remember Christ still holds the key,
Unlocks the doors to let you be
A victor any place you live,
His grace enables we forgive.
Though troubles may still get us down
We know with Him we'll never drown.
So if you're lost out on the street,
My friend, Christ Jesus you should meet.

IN CHRIST JESUS

In Christ Jesus, what's it mean?
Is it something that is seen,
Shown in ways by how we act,
Or unconnected, just a fact?
I've heard folks say that they remember
Lovingly and oh, so tender
The day their blind eyes opened up.
Spiritually God filled their cup,
And it was quickened to their soul
Christ paid the price to make them whole.
Saved by God's amazing grace
In Christ Jesus it's God's face
We see so clearly His great love;
God calls on us from up above.
In Christ Jesus, are we there?
Do we each day know His care?
Are we yielding to His direction,
Growing stronger, God's affection
Letting His light shine through us;
Getting on the Jesus bus,
Thankful deep down in our hearts
God's love to us through Christ imparts?
If it's true that Jesus saves,
Does that make us Jesus slaves?
In Christ Jesus, what's it mean?
My feeling is on Him we lean.
When we're troubled, down and out,
His Spirit will turn us about.
When our faith is all we've got,
With Jesus it is quite a lot.
When in life the troubles come,
We go to Him, He helps us some—
Enough to help us struggle through,
Revive us then and make us new.
A gracious God, this Lord of ours,
Forgiving us He heals the scars.
He puts direction in our walk
And soon will even change our talk.
In Christ Jesus we're reborn,
Not under law and all its scorn.
But we are driven to do better,
In Jesus grace, not law, each letter.
In Christ Jesus we are set free.
Sin does not have hold of me,
Nor on you if Christ is Lord.
He bids you peace, now come on board.

PURCHASE COMPLETE

Separation from the Lord,
A price we really can't afford...
It comes by sin that we have done,
These failures, guilty, everyone.
All fall short of God in glory;
This is a very human story.
Sins of action and of thought,
Shifting blame, but we cannot
Ever claim we're white as snow.
In our heart the Lord does know
The things that others may not see;
But sin abounds, may we agree.
Thus said is there a way for hope
To overcome and not just cope
With this condition of the soul,
A way in God's eyes we'd be whole?
Oh, fragile, blatant, sinner man,
God made a way that we all can
Lose ourselves from Satan's grip.
The name of Jesus does equip
Those who follow in His steps
To know the Lord in greater depth.
We'll find He wants to shine through us.
His judgments all the world can trust.
And then His love will flood you over;
His grace sufficient, fields of clover.
Sunny days with flowers bright
Can't compare when Christ is light
In the center of your being.
Repentance comes, and sin is fleeing.
Oh, temptation will remain,
But in God's love we can refrain
From giving in. A higher power
Covers us, each day, each hour.
It's in the cross which bore our shame,
Reminding us God calls our name
And says, "your purchase is complete.
Oh, come and worship at My feet."

SPECIAL PEOPLE

We're all special in God's sight,
Special people God made right.
Not perfected, nowhere near,
But no doubt one thing is clear.
Life is precious beyond measure;
The grace of God we all should treasure.
For while it's true God loves us all,
Special people sometimes fall.
Special people miss the mark,
Get lost at times, live in the dark,
And when they're lost and so in need,
God has ways their souls to feed.
God has ways to right the wrong:
A salvation plan to give us song.
Because of God's amazing grace,
Special people now can face
The Lord, the master of creation,
Confident God knows our station.
For He sent Jesus, hope of man,
As our Redeemer so we can
Find forgiveness and God's peace,
Another chance, a brand new lease.
For Jesus paid the debt in full,
The only way that He could pull
The special people He created
Close to Him. He showed we rated.
Enough to send the very best,
Our Lord will help in every test.
What makes us special all the more
Is that God waits right at the door,
Never forcing our surrender.
But when we come, so sweet and tender,
He forgives and takes us in;
He made a way to stop our sin.
We're special people all because
In Christ we know that God is love,
And we receive the gift He sent.
His love has made a big imprint.

Chapter Nine   **Victory In Jesus**

GOD HAS SPOKEN

My God has spoken to me.
My God answers prayers you see.
Mighty, powerful, yet loving is He.

Know Jesus,
He's the key.
By Him God leads us
Onward to glory, in service to Thee.

How do I know God has spoken to me?
Listen, I've changed. Glory be!
After running, God's love hooked me.

Know Jesus,
God's reflection you'll see.
Hung on a cross on a hill of dust,
Bearing my sins, He paid the fee.

No longer a gloom bug, His light shines from me.
No better Helper, Knows me to a tee,
Faults and all, He accepted me.

Know Jesus,
More loving you'll be.
Follow Him, you have His trust.
Love Him, you'll even feel glee.

God's love—on me, through me, all over me.
What a rapture! such harmony!
Thanks for the blessing in Thee.

Know Jesus,
You'll be a blessing bee.
Reaching out in love, a must.
With God's help being like He.

We are to serve others, God tells me.
A humble, contrite spirit pleases Thee.
With an eye on Jesus this can be.

Know Jesus,
A winner you'll be.
Heaven bound, no missing the bus,
And a fullness of life, that's for me!

ALPHABETICAL INDEX

1986 Year's Review	102
39th Birthday	86
A Happy Ending	17
A Holy God	108
Adopted Kids	24
All Fed Up	25
Amazed By Grace	139
Appreciation	38
As Christmas Nears	201
Autumn Blessings	166
Awakening	128
Babes In Christ	74
Being God-Centered	213
Best Of Friends	50
Blessed New Year	203
Blessed Week	39
Blunder Man	85
Bringing Comfort	178
Brother In Christ	122
Brother's Prayer	100
Call Jesus	140
Calling Cards	181
Celebrate Christ	109
Changes	55
Chicken Dinner Praise	31
Choices	175
Choir Of Bells	193
Choose Grace	47
Christian Fellowship	23
Christian Life	77
Christian Love	2
Christmas Eve Reflection	200
Christmas Once More	202
Christmas Road	197
Circle Of Love	14
Claim The Throne	82
Clean Living	129
Clover Fields	220
Compassion	92
Condition Covered	144
Confession	57
Confines	120
Consistent Love	3
Continual Care	35
Court Day	92
Day's End	153
Dependence On God	84
Discontent	67
Doing God's Work	177
Doing What We Can't	222
Don't Give Up	65
Draw Close To God	104
Drum Temper	66
Earthquake	172
Easy Living	134
Education Reflection	228
Ephesians	41
Expectations	121
Faithful Living	187
Family Of God	18
Fellowship With God	90
Flicker Faith	71
For What It's Worth	56
Forgiveness	138
Friends	31
From Head To Heart	118
Getting Real	49
Give Love	27
Go	182
God Brought Me Here	94
God Came Down	210
God Can Supply	51
God-Graced Moments	105
God Has Spoken	233
God In Season	162
God Knows	54
God Needs Women	147
Godsend	34
God Who Loves Us So	18
God Won't Leave	37
God Won't Let Go	156
God's Calling	93
God's Child	112
God's Got A Part For You	143
God's Harbor Haven	29
God's In Charge	155
God's Light	137
God's Love Is All Around	160
God's Love	5
God's Math	58
God's Mystery	37
God's New Year	204
God's Promises	46
God's Prompting	149
God's Solution	68
God's Spirit Is Living Proof	59
God's Working	20
Good Ol' Folks	114
Good Works	125
Gospel Singer	192
Grace	88
Green-Haired People	133
Growing In Amazing Grace	152
Growth In Winter	165
Hands Across America	183
Happiness	227
Hats Off To Moms	205
Heaven's Leaven	212
He's Always There	43
His Spirit Beckons Everyday	146

Title	Page
Holy Spirit	107
Holy Spirit Cooking	224
Holy Spirit, Don't Leave Me Now	62
Home	42
How Falling Leaves Relate To Me	158
Hungry Souls	209
I Can Love You	26
I Need God Every Hour	84
I Never Noticed	127
Icebergs	171
I'm Glad The Lord Loves My Soul	16
Imperfection Still God's Selection	184
In Christ Jesus	230
In Every Season	159
In God We Trust	48
In His Image	76
In One Spirit	113
It's Just A Game	40
It's Not Brainwashing	185
Jail	79
Jesus Is The Answer	28
Jesus Street	229
Jesus Train	36
Johnston City Christmas	199
Just Thinking	154
Lament	70
Law Or Grace	32
Let's Praise The Lord	214
Light Of Christmas	198
Limits	73
Live The Faith	11
Living By Faith	219
Locked Out	22
Lonely	78
Lost Girl	9
Lower Nature	63
Made Whole	132
Meeting God Together	151
Mildly Disturbed	60
Monday Evening	61
Mother-Daughter Banquet	206
Mother Earth	173
My Helper	130
New Hope Church	186
No Good Sinner	21
No Perfect People	45
Oh, How He Loves You And Me	8
On The Rocks	180
One Day I'll See Your Face	82
One Hundred Years	194
Oriented To God	150
Our Church	135
Our Life's Work	142
Out Of Debt	52
Out Of Work	64
Pardon Me	80
Peace Comes From Within	115
Peace In Jesus	218
Peace Of Mind	9
Peace With God	75
Peace	1
People God Created	4
Picking Up	42
Point of Reference	117
Positioned By God	191
Pray About It	95
Prayer For Healing	89
Prayerful Christmas	195
Prayer Time	101
Preach The Gospel Everyday. If Necessary, Use Words.	182
Problem Solver	217
Purchase Complete	231
Purposed Life	216
Quiet Time	157
Rain On	13
Reaching Out	183
Reason I Still Rhyme	226
Refreshed	124
Repentant Sinner's Heart	83
Retreat	110
Revival	81
Revival In The Camp	225
Seasons God Made	161
Simple Faith	111
Smoky	169
Snow	170
Sonlight Breaking Through	167
Special People	232
Spirit-Centered Man	123
Springtime	174
Staff Of Hope	189
Staying Close	7
Suddenly	6
Summer's End	33
Tears	44
Tell God Your Frustrations	69
Temporary Employee	30
Testimony	10
That Sunset Was Really Something	163
The Cross	221
The Devil's Lie	21
The Key	99
The Kingdom Of God	106
The Lord In My Life	215
The Love Of Christ	14
The Park	176
The Parsonage	131
The Pit	87
The Right Time	179
The River Of Life	223
The Squirrel	168

The Storm	173
The Ten Commandments	19
The Wind	164
There All Along	116
There's A Reason I Still Rhyme	226
Thirst For God	17
This Christian Life	126
This Thanksgiving Day	96
Thoughts On Prayer	91
Thoughts While Bowling	40
Time Alone	12
Time Out	174
Time With God	72
Today's Prayer	90
Touched By Jesus	208
Transparent	136
Trust In The Lord	53
Trying Times	63
Vacation	103
Vessel Of Love	119
Visions	15
Waiting Till Ready	145
We Win	148
What Christmas Means	196
What Jesus Means To Me	207
What's Done For God Just Goes Around	141
When We Feel Gritty	97
Willing Spirit	190
With Thankful Heart, Lord	98
Your Ministry	188

Made in the USA
Middletown, DE
21 March 2019